FIRST-TIME LANDLORD

A how-to-make-it-work book for new or potential landlords

Free email contact to authors!

First-Time Landlord exists to provide the new or potential landlord with basic information related to the subject of landlording and property management. It is sold with the understanding that the authors and publisher are not engaged in rendering legal, accounting, tax, or other professional services.

If legal advice or other expert assistance is required, the services of a competent professional should be sought.

✓List is a checklist of steps or items suggested by *First-Time Landlord* authors, as necessary to move ahead in the process of becoming and functioning as a landlord. Although the authors have researched and experienced a great many instances in landlord/tenant relationship there is no claim made that the offered lists will cover every landlord/tenant situation.

Side Story, Landlord Line, and Tenant Tip are used in *First-Time Landlord* as compilations of personal and professional experiences of your authors and no current or former renter is listed by their real name.

When describing specific professionals whose service a landlord may require, individuals or firms may be named. Mentioning their names is a choice of *First-Time Landlord* authors and no payment has been received from named professionals. Authors simply, to this publication date, have received excellent service from these professionals and naming them only allows for a show of appreciation - in print. Thanks!

© 2008-2010 by Wencl/Creative, Inc.

All rights reserved. The text and design of this publication, or any part thereof, may not be reproduced or stored in any manner whatsoever without written permission from the authors. In other words, without written permission of Wencl/Creative, Inc., no photocopying, scanning, recording, or duplication of any materials within *First-Time Landlord* is permitted without written permission.

Wencl/Creative, Inc.
landlordbook@wencl-creative.com

Only those who have legally purchased a copy of *First-Time Landlord* may contact authors with questions, concerns, or comments.

Dedication

We, Mike and Elaine Wencl McManigle dedicate *First-Time Landlord* to our renters, without whom we would never have written *First-Time Landlord*.

We would have had no reason, or subject matter—for that matter—without tenants.

We thank tenants who truly treat houses we offer for rent as their own homes. In *First-Time Landlord*, we don't spend enough time praising renters who respect us, and respect the property they lease from us. Truly great tenants do exist. We know.

Some of them lease a home from us.

And—if we should some day choose to end our landlord duties—we'd like our great tenants to purchase our rental properties and become landlords themselves!

Few would be interested in a book filled with stories about tenants who are both grateful and ingratiated. We did put in a few, just to show you how to spot a winner.

Good renters are winners: everyone comes out ahead. A property you own as an investment is temporarily the home for others who pay a set sum of money for a place to call their home. That's how it works successfully.

Within *First-Time Landlord* we've included warning signs and techniques to help landlords remove the other types of renters. We're talking about renters who mistreat you and your property. Read on to learn how to spot them, live with them if you must, and get rid of them as soon as possible.

Contents

Dedication iii
Acknowledgments / Foreword ix
Introduction xi

Part 1
BEFORE renters

Getting started 1
Property maintenance 1
Property management 2
Tax advantages 3
Good stuff 3
Not so good stuff 5
Think about becoming a landlord 6
Intimidation 7
Feel like a landlord 8
Landlord partners 9
Choose a rental property 11
Pay for a rental property 14
Single family, duplex, or multi-unit 15
Already a landlord 25
Meet the neighbors 25
Protect yourself 26
Advertise for tenants 26
Find renters 27
Choose tenants 27
Listen to applicants 29
Talk to applicants 29
Help applicants 30
Don't count on applicants 31
Section 8/Public Housing Assistance 33
Who's paying for what 33
Deposit for security/damage 35
Talk renters insurance 36
Submit last month's rent 37
✓List Checklist of what to do **before renters** 38
How-to-Make-it-Work Book Pages 39

BEFORE renters tab shares practical approaches to understanding how to purchase and manage a rental property.

DURING renters tab offers helpful tips and techniques to creating a good relationship between landlord and tenant.

AFTER renters tab provides a step-by-step process for ending a landlord/tenant relationship in a professional manner.

Part 2
DURING renters

DURING renters tab offers helpful tips and techniques to creating a good relationship between landlord and tenant.

New renters	45
Friendly not friends	45
Application process	46
Application Form	47
Credit Check	51
Reference Check	52
Put it in writing	53
Periodic tenancy/Month-to-month	53
Definite-Term tenancy	54
Lease	55
Take the Time	56
Initial Walk-Through	66
Clean Initial Walk-Through	66
Renters have rights	66
Landlords have rights	66
Good tenants	67
Bad tenants	67
Other tenants	68
Change the lease	68
Change the tenants	69
Change your rental property	69
Update your rental property	70
Landlords at rental property	71
Tenants at landlord's other property	71
✓List Checklist of what to do **during renters**	72
How-to-Make-it-Work Book Pages	73

Part 3
AFTER renters

Unexpected end of Lease	79
Reason to end a Lease	82
End of Lease Notice	84
Lease End	84
Eviction	85
Unlawful Detainer	86
Court	87
Good tenants leave	88
Bad tenants leave	88
Other tenants leave	88
No forwarding address	90
Final Walk-Through	90
Final Clean Walk-Through	91
Reference Calls	92
Follow-Up Letter	93
Return of Security/Damage Deposit	94
Return of Security/Damage Deposit Interest	94
Deductible Expenses	95
Before you consider new tenants	96
In Closing	97
✓List Checklist of what to do **after renters**	98
How-to-Make-it-Work Book Pages	99

Index

A reference list of terms used in *First-Time Landlord*	105

AFTER renters tab provides a step-by-step process for ending a landlord/tenant relationship in a professional manner.

Acknowledgments

We want to thank our family and friends who have had such patience with us as we journey through our professional landlord career.

We don't know why you've been so patient with us—but we appreciate it every day and night!

Throughout *First-Time Landlord* we have acknowledged some of the fantastic advice we've received from those who care if we succeed as landlords, or maybe they just want us (more specifically Elaine) to stop talking!

As writers we know what we want to share. But without proofreaders we don't know if we've really reached our goal. Thank you to our dear friend Janice Eileen Hanson Holmberg for serving as our first proofreader.

Our final proofreaders include a very good friend (see we didn't add your name) and our geographically closest family members: Bill, Pat, and Mandy Inhofer. No words can describe the depth of our appreciation.

Finally, we want to thank Erika Rinkleff Photography for allowing us to include one of our favorite photos…

Mike and Elaine,

First-Time Landlord Authors

Foreword

As *First-Time Landlord*'s proofreader I found *First-Time Landlord* enlightening.

I have considered becoming a landlord—now I'd know how to do it!
I've learned so much helpful information— thanks Mike and Elaine!

Janice Hanson Holmberg

Introduction

In late 2002, Mike and Elaine Wencl McManigle decided to buy rental property. Elaine tried to find a truly basic book for new landlords. She couldn't find it. Without the research they needed, Mike and Elaine boldly began to buy rental property.

Today they own and manage five rental units. Now they have the hands-on experience to create just what Elaine wanted back in 2002: *First-Time Landlord*.

Risky Business

Everything in life is a risk.

You may have been told it's a simple process and takes no effort on a landlord's part. Suggestions like this only describe landlords who don't care about their rental property.

If you care, it shows.

Free email contact to authors

Feel free to email us at landlordbook@wencl-creative.com with your landlord and/or tenant questions, comments, and concerns. Be prepared to provide proof of *First-Time Landlord* book purchase. Unlimited emails—contact us!

Side Story

Throughout *First-Time Landlord* your authors include examples of various situations. As a landlord, you may be able to avoid a more difficult situation by taking care of a problem before it escalates into a more difficult situation.

Learn from Mike and Elaine's sometimes embarrassing but always educational experiences.

Added to enhance the learning experience, a Side Story will appear in a sidebar. Sometimes it's as simple as explaining why "Mike/Elaine keep a list of potential tenants who have not shown up for a scheduled appointment."

Take What You Need

First-Time Landlord is written so that each part can stand alone:

BEFORE renters covers from purchasing rental property through the moment you are ready for renters to move in,

DURING renters covers the time period when renters occupy your property, and

AFTER renters covers from time renters are about to vacate, or have vacated, your rental.

Read *First-Time Landlord* from front to back, or just refer to the sections that cover your immediate needs.

Remember, information provided within this text is not legal advice and you should refer to a professional whenever you need services.

How-to-Make-it-Work Book Pages

First-Time Landlord is purposely built with lots of additional blank space to create your own calculations, write notes, or remind yourself of critical information. Think of it as a how-to-make-it-work book, where you can record the information you need to make your landlord responsibilities easier.

Computer with Internet Connection

Before we go any further, we need to explain a landlord needs a computer with internet access. Besides keeping current on government rental housing law, you need access to online credit checks. We sometimes even use a search engine to find public information about potential tenants. Information helps.

Tenant Tip

Throughout all three parts of *First-Time Landlord* you will find Tenant Tips. Based on Mike/Elaine's experience, Tenant Tips are included as short cuts to right choices with tenants. A tip can seem so logical, after the fact. Sometimes a Tenant Tip is this basic, "In the last month of rental, deliver to the tenant a reminder that they need to complete a final walk-through with you. Perhaps you'd rather set a time when you'll be at the property or require them to schedule an appointment with you. Final walk-throughs must be done, or the tenant may claim they left the unit in great shape."

Landlord Line

Throughout all three parts of *First-Time Landlord* you will find Landlord Lines. Successful landlords do not win popularity contests because they must enforce regulations. Sometimes the regulations are of their own creation. Sometimes it's just remembering to tell them simple Landlord Lines like, "You signed a lease saying no pets are allowed, your Great Dane cannot live here with you." Landlord Lines encourage you to stick to your agreement with renters, "No, your five brothers and sisters cannot move in with you, our lease states this is a one-bedroom apartment and only two people may reside here."

✓List

A checklist is steps or items suggested by *First-Time Landlord* authors, as helpful to move ahead in the process of becoming and functioning as a landlord. Although the authors have researched and experienced a great many instances in landlord/tenant relationship there is no claim made that the offered lists will cover every landlord/tenant situation.

First-Time Landlord, Second Edition

Feel free to email us at landlordbook@wencl-creative.com if you have questions you'd like answered. If we don't know the answer, we will offer you some direction or at least respond to your email.

Our only requirement: you must have legally purchased a copy of our book *First-Time Landlord*, First Edition, to receive our email service.

If you send us an email, please understand you are giving us the legal right to use the topic you have introduced in *First-Time Landlord*, Second Edition. That is, if we choose to create a second, updated version. If we use your communication, we would list your name as a contributor and change the names of all other parties involved.

Part 1
BEFORE renters

Getting started

Nothing is ever as simple as it sounds. Neither is being a landlord.
Our goal is to walk you through the process of becoming, and being, a landlord. If you are already a landlord, you can skip to "Already a landlord" (See page 25) but you might be interested in what we believe is good and bad about being a landlord. Read on if you like.

Property maintenance

We might as well get this out of the way. Property maintenance is the physical work involved in maintaining a rental unit. Legally, you cannot be paid to maintain your own property. What?

If you clean a home before new renters take possession you cannot be paid for your time. This is called property maintenance and if you were to pay yourself, you could charge whatever you want. So, you can charge nothing.

Your compensation is a rental home that is ready to be re-rented without out-of-pocket expense except for the supplies and materials you had to purchase to maintain your rental property.

Tenant Tip

Sometimes property maintenance involves others—like your rental property neighbors.

Mike/Elaine expect tenants who rent our single-family property to complete their own yardwork. Sometimes they don't.

If Mike sees the gardens in bad shape, he just gets into his property maintenance mode. Mike starts weeding. Suddenly the tenant comes out to help weed—but only when Mike's already started the project!

BEFORE renters

Tenant Tip

Speaking of damage caused by tenants, Mike/Elaine do not always required renters to pay for damage as they cause it. Elaine will remind them that specific damage will need to eventually be repaired. It's best to remind tenants that damage expenses will be deducted from their security/damage deposit.

Side Story

Mike/Elaine have paid off their house. They're sitting on the biggest hunk of money they've ever seen.

Looking for additional work and extra income, they decide to refinance their house and buy a rental property; then maybe another one.

You can hire anyone you like and pay them whatever you want, but remember that expense is deducted from your profit.

If your renter has purposely damaged your rental property you can charge them for the repair. You must advise them of this beforehand; placing it in your contract is a great idea. You could also include a clause about unexplained damage, where it cannot be proven how the damage occurred. We split the cost with the renter – 50/50 – in those cases. Remember, you cannot charge them for your own time.

If your renter reports damage considered normal wear and tear, you cannot charge them. It was not their fault. You must repair or replace it at your own expense.

If you cannot prove a renter was neglectful or created the problem, do not expect compensation from your renter. If you cannot show proof, they don't have to accept blame.

You may or may not know it, but this is not the same as property maintenance. Property maintenance is brawn or muscle, while property management is the brains. Legally – as an individual – you cannot be paid to manage your property. But, done properly, your rental property will earn income for you...

As far as we understand, you cannot manage anyone else's property except for your own, without a realtor license. Legally you can manage your own property, but no one else's without being a realtor with a legal realtor license.

Financially, you must provide at least these three things: a mortgage, if you have one; property taxes; and homeowners insurance.

All three will be discussed at length throughout First-Time Landlord.

Tax advantages

Paying taxes is part of life. But owning rental property has so many tax advantages that it needs to be mentioned separately.

Tax deductions are very nice too, but make sure you hire a qualified tax preparer. Why?

Professional tax preparers pay for expensive tax software that provides them the latest tax deductions. Tax laws change continuously. You may be able to receive more tax benefits. If you don't know the latest federal and state tax provisions you are doing two things: losing out on the most current updates and leaving yourself open for legal problems if the government should choose to audit your taxes.

Good stuff

Invest. It's a good way to make money, but you need to keep control. Do you know the difference between mutual funds and stocks, in basic terms? With mutual funds you "invest" as part of a group, with stocks you "invest" by owning a share of the business. Rather than being part of a group, or a shareholder, invest in property as another way to increase your financial stability.

Rental property is an investment. That's a good thing. If real estate is increasing in value, your investment grows. If real estate is decreasing in value, just hold on to your property. Maybe even buy more, if you are financially sound. One way or another, real estate is sound investment—if you stay with it.

Tenants can be part of the good stuff. Mike and Elaine disagree regarding tenants.

Mike dislikes communicating with tenants. Elaine enjoys meeting new people, so she's got lots to share. Here's the catch: if you don't like dealing with people you're not going to like the people part of landlording. If you can, hire someone you trust to find your renters, deal with them, and save you the grief. But someone has to do it.

Side Story

Jeanne and John want to invest some extra savings. They'd like some extra tax deductions. Jeanne and John find a 50's decorated house in their neighborhood at way below market value, and jump at the chance to buy it and earn some extra income as landlords – maybe just for a few years.

Side Story

Will and Cathy work over an hour from home. They buy a new house closer to their jobs, but suddenly a half-dozen houses in their old neighborhood are for sale. Cathy suggests rather than offer their house at a sacrifice price, why not wait until the market is better – and rent out their old home for awhile.

BEFORE renters

Side Story

Sadly, Marty's grandma died. Marty inherited her home, a cute little bungalow. He moved into the house, but now Marty's getting married and wants to move into his bride's larger house. He's not ready to say good-bye to Grandma's house so Marty chooses to rent it out – just for awhile.

Because Elaine likes the people part of rental, she considers it a good part of being a landlord: giving people the opportunity to create a home.

Mike likes taking care of property, improving it. Consider rehabbing a house, creating a safe and secure home. It's good to take on property that is basically sound, but hasn't been treated with care.

Hey, Mike is like Elaine.

Elaine likes to give people a good start in a nice house.

Mike likes to give a house a nice start as a good home!

What would you consider to be good points about owning rental property?

Right now, put your thoughts here. In a few months or a few years, if you decide to become a landlord, return here to see what your thoughts were.

Becoming a landlord, what would you consider to be the benefits? Are you ready?

Not-so-good stuff

We agree there is some not so good stuff.

Here goes: your money is tied up in rental property; you need to keep extra money for repairs/maintenance; and most importantly: you are now responsible for providing a rental unit that is a family's home.

You are responsible for their shelter and somewhat for their protection. Unless you pay someone else to take over that responsibility, you now need to be available for their emergencies and leave them access to you for non-emergencies.

What would you consider to be not-so-good stuff about owning rental property? Right now, put your thoughts here. In a few minutes, months or years, if you decide to become a landlord return here to see what your thoughts were.

Becoming a landlord, what would you consider not-so-good stuff?

BEFORE renters

Think about becoming a landlord

By now you probably know if you're capable of being a landlord. But remember a landlord has control over the most basic part of a person's life: where they live. Power lies there. Don't abuse it.

Being a landlord is like having children – without the love. Well, okay, you can grow to love renters. But don't let it show. Well, most of the time.

If you're a successful landlord, you'll never win a popularity contest. You can never please all your renters, all the time. You'd be giving them free rent, and pocket money too!

Be fair to your renters. Give them a good place to live, respect their privacy, and expect them to give you the same respect in return.

Lots of reasons exist to consider becoming a landlord.

Your reason, or reasons, to consider becoming a landlord can be similar or quite different from our side stories.

Make a list here, of why you'd like to become a landlord. Come on, it'll take a moment but in a few months or a few years you may be surprised why you chose to become a property manager.

Why would I like to be a landlord?

Intimidation

Intimidation is using force of some sort against another person to make them compliant to your wishes or interests.

Basically, it is attempting to make another person timid and responsive to your demands.

Intimidation is a landlord telling a potential tenant that if they don't fill out an application today the rental property will not be available, even though it is obvious the potential applicant has mixed feelings about the rental property or location.

Intimidation is a tenant demanding a landlord must allow additional people to live in the rental unit, more pets, or extend their lease against the landlord's wishes.

Intimidation is a powerful weapon. Landlords and tenants can both use it. But to be successful, the other has to be intimidated. Avoid intimidation; it has a nasty side effect.

Landlord Line

Say, "We don't feel this will work out." Intimidation is a two-way street. We have been told—by a family member who would like to remain unidentified—to "never rent to anyone you cannot intimidate." If you find yourself easily intimidated by others, you'll have a hard time as a landlord.

Do I find myself easily intimidated by others, or do I actually enjoy standing up for what is fair?

Side Story

Lyle and Laurie, as a married couple, weren't good applicants. Laurie had good references, but Lyle was in his thirties and his work record only went back six months. Six months! On top of that, Laurie proudly claimed a former renter of Mike/Elaine's, Maria, as a close friend of hers. That cinched it, because Maria had been a horrible renter. Lyle and Laurie, with their completed application in hand and without calling first, drove to your authors' home and knocked on the door. Peeking out a window, Elaine saw it was Lyle and Laurie. What did grown-up Mike/Elaine do?

They hid in their backyard, so they couldn't hear Lyle and Laurie's persistent door knocking and doorbell ringing.

While in their backyard, Elaine called one of her favorite brothers and explained the embarrassing situation. Her brother reminded Elaine that as landlords they had the right to say "We don't feel this will work out." And that's exactly what Mike/Elaine did. Lyle and Laurie went away. Mike/Elaine have never since been afraid to say, "We don't feel this will work out."

BEFORE renters

BEFORE renters

Tenant Tip

Mike/Elaine received a call from a friend who is truly like family. Her son and his family were being evicted. The friend was asking if Mike/Elaine had a unit open.

Mike/Elaine did not but if they had they definitely would have considered providing the friend's son and his family with a home.

Mike/Elaine knew the friend would help out with rent if needed.

Consider accepting tenants to whom you are related—or almost related—and do consider a co-signer on the lease if you have concerns the tenant may have trouble submitting rent.

Feel like a landlord

Do you have good friends? If you are lucky enough to have people around you that you call friends, consider what makes your relationships work.

Ever hear about the conversations people start with a doctor at a party? They want help, advice, and to save a medical bill.

As a landlord, keep your professional and personal relationship separate—whenever you can.

A family member or a friend may call you in desperation needing a place to rent. You're doing them the best favor if you help them get in somewhere else. Don't put family or friends in your investment rental property unless it is an exceptional circumstance. We'll discuss possible situations in a bit.

Family and friends know they are special to you. Not planning to do so they make take advantage of your relationship. When it comes time to pay rent they may ask for a little extra time or some extra favors. Keep your professional rental separate from your personal friends and family. Unless you're a glutton for punishment.

We have never rented to family or friends but it doesn't mean we never will. Really! It would only be short term or simply an emergency. You want to keep your family close, but not that close. You also want to keep your friends on a friendly basis with you!

What do you think makes for a good landlord? Take a moment to put your thoughts here. Come back later, in a few months or few years to see if your feelings have changed.

Landlord Partners

Are you considering being a solo landlord without a partner or adding someone to equally share the responsibilities with you? If so, consider keeping to the personal and professional separation we just mentioned.

Do you have a partner, or plan to add one? Your partner and you may have a strictly professional relationship, or it could be your spouse.

Do you and your partner have equal rights? Are you both sharing the responsibility? If so you need to decide before you even interview your first potential tenant—who has more responsibility and/or decision making power. Consider all possible situations.

It is unlikely that you and your partner, or partners, will agree on absolutely everything. You will have differences.

If your landlord partner is your significant other, spouse, or just a friend - you must attempt to keep your professional and personal relationships separate. If you share a home, try to keep areas of the home "off limits" for discussing your landlord duties.

See the next page for photos of your authors, before and after they became landlords.

If you have a landlord partner, how will your duties be shared? Who will have the decision making power in each area of responsibility?

Side Story

James and Anne were fairly new to landlording. Anne felt sympathy for Crystal, a new tenant and wanted to allow Crystal exceptions that their other tenants were not allowed. James wanted to take a firm stand and Anne would not agree. Months later Crystal moved out without notice - and left one ton (yes 1,000 pounds) of trash and debris inside the house. Anne and James fought over Crystal from the beginning to the end of Crystal's tenancy.

Side Story

Mike/Elaine agree they have equal say over landlord decisions. But because Mike does almost all the property maintenance, Elaine agrees Mike should have the final choice on tenants. It's that simple: Mike's going to see them more!

BEFORE renters

Landlord Partners

Landlord partners need to represent themselves as one unit: tenants may be confused if they receive mixed messages from their landlords.

Mike and Elaine before becoming landlords.

Tenant Tip

Don't confuse your tenants. Set rules and then abide by them. If two or more of you share landlord duties make sure you are not sending mixed messages. Landlord from one head - not two or more heads!

Mike/ Elaine after becoming landlords.

Tenants can become frustrated if one landlord allows certain activities and another landlord forbids the same actions. In reality, Mike/Elaine have found tenants can enjoy "good landlord/bad landlord" situations where one landlord has a more friendly attitude than the other landlord. But, when it comes to your policies stand together. Don't confuse your tenants. Stick by the policies you have set in place.

Choose a rental property

Let's talk about what you want in a rental property.

Do you want it nearby, or distant; cheap or nice (usually you cannot get both); and a single-family or multi-family property?

If you're going to buy a rental property, let's walk you through the process: what will make you money; what will cost you money?

To decide if a rental property can make you a profit, you need to calculate all your expenses and the rental income you can earn in your target neighborhood.

Your goal should be a property that can give you a profit: you can rent it and not lose money.

If you are new to the area or don't know the city in which you are considering buying investment property, we suggest an online search at: www.city-data.com. With First-Time Landlord going to print, the website currently includes a great deal of critical information. Included is an estimator that gives a low- and high-level estimate for possible purchase price of a specific home. Check it out!

Police

If you don't live in the community in which you are considering purchasing rental property or you are just researching a community, consider making a visit to the local police station. Ask questions about the area. The police may or may not be helpful, but at least you'll know how to find the police station!

Local Stores

Consider checking out the local stores. Focus more on convenience locations as you want to ask people working there about the community. The worst that can happen is you learn things you really didn't want to know. Like the area is famous for drug use. Now that would be a red flag. You never know, you could also find your first renters.

Side Story

Mike/Elaine have dear friends, Fred and June, who own a small house in a small city near a large city. June and Fred used to call that house home, but now they live a few states away. So they rent their former home.

Since Mike is good at rehabbing homes and Mike/Elaine have rental properties - June and Fred offered their former home to Mike/Elaine at a significantly reduced price. Elaine went online to www.city-data.com and discovered it would not be a good investment for them. Fred and June have had the same renter for decades and didn't realize that over the years close to 20% of the homes are now unoccupied which would leave Mike/Elaine with a significantly reduced renter pool. Research your target area and target population.

www.city-data.com

BEFORE renters

BEFORE renters

Tenant Tip

Don't think of tenant rental income as your mortgage payments. Your money source - to cover your mortgage payments - needs to be separate. Another way; don't depend on this month's rental payments to cover next month's mortgage.

It's too risky!

Calculate the price of a rental property

Even before you look for property, you should check the classifieds for current rentals. What's the rent? If rent for a three bedroom single-family home is $1,000, what can you afford to pay for a home and break even? Here's a cool calculation Elaine learned from her first favorite brother: Steve. Steve doesn't' claim he made this up – but it's a good calculation tool.

Steve says one year's rent (without calculating expenses) should equal one-tenth of the home's purchase price. In ten years, without expenses, a profitable rental home should pay for itself.

Here's an example: We paid $220,000 for a duplex in 2003. At that time, each unit paid $1,000 in rent, without including utilities. With duplexes and twelve months in a year here's the calculation:

$220,000 (purchase price)
$1,000 (each unit monthly rent) X 2 (two units) = $2,000 per month
$2,000 X 12 (months in a year) = $24,000.

Using those figures, we have a return (before expenses remember) of $24,000 per year – more than one-tenth their purchase price of $220,000. Now, keeping units rented every month of the year is another challenge!

Do your own calculation. Use this space to complete your own profit/loss. Remember you may have other variables involved; just consider this a starting point:

$_____ (purchase price)
$_____ (each unit monthly rent) X _____ (number of units) =
$ (A) _____ per month
$(A from above) _____ X 12 (months in a year) = $_____
(Remember this final figure optimally should be at least 10% of your purchase price.)

Here's more opportunities to calculate if a rental property is a good investment.

Use this space to complete your own profit/loss. Remember you may have other variables involved; just consider this a starting point:

$_____ (purchase price)
$_____ (each unit monthly rent) X ____ (number of units) =
$ (A) _____ per month
$(A from above) _____ X 12 (months in a year) = $_____
(Remember this final figure optimally should be at least 10% of your purchase price.)

Use this space to complete your own profit/loss. Remember you may have other variables involved; just consider this a starting point:

$_____ (purchase price)
$_____ (each unit monthly rent) X ____ (number of units) =
$ (A) _____ per month
$(A from above) _____ X 12 (months in a year) = $_____
(Remember this final figure optimally should be at least 10% of your purchase price.)

Use this space to complete your own profit/loss. Remember you may have other variables involved; just consider this a starting point:

$_____ (purchase price)
$_____ (each unit monthly rent) X ____ (number of units) =
$ (A) _____ per month
$(A from above) _____ X 12 (months in a year) = $_____
(Remember this final figure optimally should be at least 10% of your purchase price.)

BEFORE renters

Tenant Tip

As a landlord you may have more options if you personally own a rental property, rather than own it through a business.

Your tenants, in most states we know, can only be your family if you own the rental property. For instance, if you operate a rental property—but the actual ownership of the property is through a business you own—you cannot rent the property to your nephew.

Consider personally owning your investment property because it is then your rental and you can rent to whomever you want as a tenant.

Remember, seek out legal assistance before determining what is best for you.

Pay for a rental property

You have to pay for a rental property, unless a rich relative has given it to you. Now, that would be nice, but for the rest of us we have to figure out a legal way to purchase our rental property.

You do not need to own a home, to purchase a rental property. Really! If your rental situation is satisfactory, you could consider becoming a landlord, while you're still a tenant. Beware though, if you are planning on applying for a mortgage you'll likely get a much better interest rate if it's a home you plan to live in and not a rental property.

Are you interested in purchasing a duplex and living in one of the units for a few years? We know people who have done that with success. But your neighbors are going to be next door. If they want to complain, you're right there.

Same thing applies if you want to purchase the house next to yours. You would likely treat a neighbor differently than a renter.

Let's talk ownership.

Financially, you can personally own a rental property. If you borrowed money to purchase it by obtaining a mortgage you can be named as the mortgagee. It's your investment and yours to do with as you like. After six months or a year you can sell your property if you own it personally. Remember, if you have definite-length leases you are required to declare this information to your buyer. But the property is yours.

If you like, plans can be made to have a limited liability corporation (LLC) purchase the property. You, your family, or friends can own an LLC and manage your property through the firm.

We strongly recommend you arrange for an LLC with a legal professional. Be aware though, the rental property conditions of ownership are different. Complete a great deal of research before you choose the LLC route. Legally your options may be different; for example you may not be able to rent your property to a family member.

Renting to a family member, now that's a choice we have never made. But we never say never. We talk more about that elsewhere.

If you own and live in the home you plan to use as rental property, consider your options. Do you already have a home mortgage? If so, your interest rate is likely lower than any other interest rate you will be offered by a legitimate lender.

Single family, duplex, or multi-unit

It may sound like a complicated choice, but whether you choose a single family, duplex, or multi-unit rental property as an investment is relatively simple. What can you afford to maintain? Don't over extend yourself.

Here's partial lists of possible advantages and disadvantages to various rental property options. **We've repeated advantages and disadvantages, as they relate to each option.** The biggest concerns we've found are: yard care, utilities, and distance. We've separated them so you can compare the same concerns.

Single Family Advantages

- **Yard Care.** Possibly the biggest advantage of a one-family property is that it is easier to require the tenant to take care of the lawn care and snow removal, if required.

- **Utilities.** Unless your situation is unusual, renters should be responsible for payment of their own utilities: gas, electric, sewer, water, and possibly trash pickup. We include city based billings which could include street lights and more.

- **Distance.** Let's not forget that unless you live next door or in the neighborhood, your tenant is not likely to come and visit you unannounced. You are less convenient to them. That could be nice.

BEFORE renters

Tenant Tip

As landlord you may receive a citation or other government documents at your investment property. Be on good terms with your tenant - we thought we were - but we found U.S.P.O. mailings - addressed to us in the rental property...after the tenant moved out!

Specifically applying to single family or duplex properties don't expect all governing offices to have your home/business address!

Single Family Disadvantages

- **Yard Care.** If your single family house is vacant, with no tenant, you are responsible for yard care.

  When you have tenants you may or may not have them take care of the yard. If they are paying for utilities including water, they may not water the lawn. Then the grass dies. If the grass grows, renters may not mow it. Grass left without trimming will continue to grow, surprise! If your rental property is within a town or city limits there could be regulations on lawn grass height.

  You could receive a citation or fine for grass left to grow tall. If the paperwork is mailed to the rental property, the renters probably won't alert you and pretty soon the city will be out mowing your lawn - charging you for the cost. It may be months or years before you realize who has really been mowing your lawn. With the tenants perhaps even gone, you'll be left to pay for your lawn mowing!

- **Utilities.** If your single family house is vacant, you must pay for all the basic utilities: water, sewer, gas, and electric unless you choose to turn off some of these utilities. If you turn off/deactivate a utility, just to turn it back on when your unit is occupied, other costs are incurred including a set up or installation fee. Check out hidden expenses.

  When your unit is occupied, renters may simply choose to not pay their utilities. Legally the utility firms providing the services cannot share with you information about your tenants. They cannot tell if your tenants are paying the utility bills. In most cases you, as landlord, are not going to be held responsible for unpaid utilities but you should check. In our communities, we are held responsible for unpaid water bills. You may be responsible for other unpaid utilities or services provided to your rental property. Check with your local city and utility providers.

- **Distance.** If your rental property is not near your home, it's much more inconvenient for you to drive by the house you're renting out to see if the lawn is mowed and sidewalks are kept clean. Remember, if your renters don't think you'll check up on them they may not take care of your investment property.

Our biggest rental challenges have come in our single family rental home. We think distance is our biggest problem. We live about an hour away from the rental house. Tenants don't always seem to realize we will check up on them. Our list of disadvantages to single-family home rentals may continue to grow!

Duplex Advantages

Our most successful form of rental property, we have found is our duplexes. We imagine some of the same advantages would hold true for triplexes and fourplexes.

- **Yard Care.** Lawn care and snow removal, if required, are bigger issues when you have more than one rental unit on your property. You have options, which will be discussed under *Duplex Disadvantages*, but you must have consistent lawn care. At least for other residents in your rental property neighborhood, you should maintain good lawn care. You don't need a great yard - with flowers and the latest landscaping - but provide a good and attractive yard.

- **Utilities.** At least in our state, it is illegal to require one renter to pay for another renter's utilities. Therefore, if utilities in the separate units are not individually billable (separate meters) you cannot expect one renter to pay all the utilities. If one utility bill is shared by more than one unit, we pay the utility ourselves and give renters a rebate incentive. Basically they pay for their own utilities, but submit at least a portion of the utility with their monthly rent. We cover this later in Part 1:

Side Story

Mike provides all the yard care, including lawn mowing, of Mike/Elaine's duplex properties. Mike/Elaine purchased a second duplex that is within a quarter mile of their first duplex. Because of an existing conditional use permit in place, Mike/Elaine had to attend city hall meetings where the neighbors were invited to come and discuss Mike/Elaine's pending purchase of the new property.

At the city hall meeting, a neighbor who lives between the properties stood and said that he liked the way Mike/Elaine took care of their rental property, and he wanted them to buy the second property. Mike/Elaine liked hearing that keeping their rental property yard in good condition was also keeping their neighbors happy.

BEFORE renters

Side Story

Mike/Elaine received a call from Mark, who rented one of Mike/Elaine's duplexes. He called to tell us Terry and Karen, our renters next door had been fighting the night before, police had been called, and now one of the renters was moving out. Mike/Elaine showed up to find Karen packing up all her possessions and moving out. She was mad at Terry and thought she could just walk away from her contract with us. Sometimes it pays to have a renter next door to another renter!

BEFORE Renters in section Who's paying for what. Check it out and see if it'll work for you. You are ensuring the utilities are paid, by paying the bills yourself. Calculate your monthly rent payments to include the utilities. Requiring renters to pre-submit for their utilities is an advantage, because you know the bills are being paid.

- **Distance.** Living close or far from your rental property doesn't have a significant advantage when looking at a duplex rental property. The distance advantage comes into play for your renters.

  The possibly biggest advantage we have found to owning a duplex is that you have renters living near to each other.

  Not all tenants, but some love to tattle on the other and they'll call you if someone is moving out in the middle of the night. Or just to lie about the other tenants - so you'll like them better! By the way, don't encourage them to tell you everything your other tenants are doing - tattling for petty reasons is not a desirable behavior.

Duplex Disadvantages

We have found fewer bad things about having more than one rental unit on the same property.

- **Yard Care.** The biggest disadvantage is trash left in the yard. If you have more than one tenant, they may leave cans, fast food wrappers, and other discards in your rental yard and blame it on the other tenant. A bigger concern is going to be who takes care of the yard.

  Here are some options:

  You could take care of the yard. Lawn mowing, care of any gardens, and snow removal, if needed, could be provided by you. Falling under property maintenance, you know the neighbors would like your rental property looking good - but you cannot bill or get paid for the service you provide. You own the property; you cannot be paid to maintain the property.

You could hire a contractor, a friend or reliable lawn care provider, to mow the lawn and/or maintain the yard. Snow removal, if required, could be handled the same way. Pay whomever provides this service at least the current rate in your area. Friend or contractor, you want them to take good care of your yard. Include the amount you calculate you will have to pay for lawn service in your costs, along with mortgage (if any), property taxes, and house insurance.

A tenant, either living in your rental property or another property you own, could provide the lawn services. Check with your renter information provider before choosing the route of leaving a renter responsible for lawn care. If you pay them, or reduce their rent by having them mow, you may possibly have to consider them an employee. That means you could end up paying taxes based on their work. We've had renters offer to mow the lawn - for free. Consider passing on that option too. How long would you mow the lawn for free?

- **Utilities.** If utilities are metered separately into each rental unit it is most practical and efficient to have each tenant responsible for their own utilities. As we've mentioned elsewhere, some utilities - if left unpaid - could become your responsibility. It is not unusual, if your city bills for water usage, and the water bill goes unpaid that they could add this amount to your property taxes.

    If utilities are shared as we describe in utility incentive, some renters could carelessly overuse utilities and other renters would end up paying more than their share. If an uncaring renter purposely leaves their windows open while using air conditioning, a significant waste of utilities could be incurred. The best option is to choose tenants wisely and verbally impress on new renters that they are sharing utilities.

If you provide laundry facilities that more than one rental unit must share, consider the possibility of purchasing and installing coin-operated equipment. If you find yourself cleaning the laundry facility at least you'll be earning some extra income. In this case, as your own property maintenance you can keep this income. But do realize you must report money earned—just like any other rental income.

- **Distance.** Once again, disadvantages described are more so about your tenants sharing a property but within separate units. One renter can call you and share truths, or untruths, about another renter that you don't necessarily want to know. Once again, it's a good idea to carefully screen your renters when they are sharing a property, but living in separate units.

    As long as renters are living in separate units you should never force your individual tenants to work out their differences. This could lead to unhappy results. You may have to mediate. Never require renters - living in separate units - to resolve their problems without your input because you could be held responsible for any violence or damage that may occur. Simply, it's not nice.

    You chose both of them as tenants, therefore you are responsible to keep a livable relationship between your renters.

Multi-Unit Advantages

We do not own any units larger than duplexes, although we did make an offer on a triplex. When we discuss multi-units, we are discussing small or larger apartment buildings, probably a four-plex building or larger.

We did research multi-units when purchasing our rental properties. We've also talked to others who own multi-unit properties. Once again, we would refer to four-plexes or apartment buildings as multi-unit properties.

A huge advantage to multi-unit rental properties is that all units do not have to be rented for you to make a profit. Let's say there are eight units, to break even you should be able to have a vacancy in at least one unit.

- **Yard Care.** You must provide all lawn care by completing the service yourself or hiring a contractor. Because you are holding no renter responsible for the lawn mowing, you know the property will look good.

    Remember, once again, if you mow the lawn or prune the bushes you cannot receive pay for this. You cannot be paid for providing your own property maintenance.

- **Utilities.** You must pay for all utilities. You know all utilities are being paid, because that's your responsibility. Make sure to calculate for any change in utility cost changes when determining monthly rents. Separate units, within a multi-unit property, can be held responsible for their utilities only if there are individual meters to each unit. No renter should be responsible for the utilities of a renter living in a separate unit. If no separate meters exist for the units you need to consider a form of sharing the utility expense. You may want to consider the square footage of the unit or number of rooms in each unit, if they differ in size.

- **Distance.** Like duplexes, the distance we are referring to here is not particularly the distance between your rental unit and your personal home. The distance we want to discuss is the physical space between renters.

    In a multi-unit property, like an apartment building, a great many special issues are a concern but if designed/monitored well, they can be considered advantages:

BEFORE renters

Side Story

A multi-unit concern, Mike/Elaine purchased a building that has two separate homes. When they purchased the home, Mike/Elaine were required to remove an interior door which had been previously installed in a common wall area between the two homes. County regulations required Mike/Elaine to install a fire-door. When purchasing or inspecting a multi-unit rental property make sure you address concerns involving multi-unit properties. If you later have a problem it's always best to have proof you had the property inspected and regulations are met, or exceeded.

Sound protection between each unit - based on age of building this could be an issue; if building is well constructed good sound buffering should be between walls and floor/ceilings.

Shared facilities like laundry and outside yard/garden spaces should be well lit and kept neat and tidy. If these areas are not kept in good condition, tenants will not feel they need to respect the areas.

Last, but definitely not least are your renters themselves. An advantage to closely spaced rental units - as in an apartment building - is that if a renter is doing some illegal or disruptive to your other renters - other renters are nearby to alert you of the bad renter actions!

Do remind all tenants - their well being is most important! If they overhear or see something illegal they should alert the police first. Next they should call you.

Multi-Unit Disadvantages

We do not own any units larger than duplexes, but researched multi-units when purchasing our rental properties. We've also talked to others who own multi-unit properties. We would refer to four-plexes or apartment buildings as multi-unit properties.

A huge disadvantage to multi-unit rental properties is your start up costs. Larger properties, obviously, cost more money. Consider too, maintenance and repair concerns with heating, plumbing, and electrical. Can you afford to repair or even replace the furnace? If not, you should rethink a larger rental property like an apartment building. You are responsible for the upkeep, care, and maintenance for multiple units.

- **Yard Care.** You must pay for all the yard care, or provide it yourself without receiving payment. If you mow the lawn of your apartment building you will not have the expense of paying someone else to mow it. But your renters may leave trash in the yard, because it is not their yard and they know you will likely not know for sure who left the trash.

- **Utilities.** You must pay for all utilities. If all renters are being billed the same amount for a shared utility, you can only hope they are not careless and leave windows open when air conditioning is being used or overuse any appliances within the unit. You may be surprised to find out a tenant is operating a bakery out of a rental unit kitchen. Baking three dozen loaves of bread every day can drive a utility use up very quickly. The more rental units you have, the more chance to abuse and overuse. Watch for utility abuse and control it immediately.

- **Distance.** One of the biggest disadvantages to a multi-unit rental property, as we see it, is with more rental units it is harder to control. If you live nearby, you may receive many unscheduled visits from various renters. They may want to complain about other renters in your unit, complain about how you treat them or other renters in your unit, or simply visit. As we've mentioned elsewhere, curb these unscheduled visits to your home by visiting politely for a few minutes and then announce you must leave. Then lock up your house and leave. Renters who like to drop in on their landlords will soon learn they are only welcome when they have real concerns and issues.

  In a multi-unit property like an apartment building, the same special issues that are advantages can be disadvantages:

  Sound protection between each unit - if building was not well constructed there will be little or no buffer. Consider adding sound barrier. Check doors. At a minimum consider twenty-minute fire doors to help improve sound protection and safety.

- Shared facilities like laundry, outside yard/garden spaces easily could become untidy. Unattractive shared areas

BEFORE renters

Side Story

James and Anne own a duplex with a shared laundry. Some renters are neat and tidy, even cleaning up other renters' messes. Though good tenants like that are wonderful, they don't discourage bad renters who make messes.

At some point, if James and Anne once again have tenants that don't clean up their own messes, James will install a coin-operated washer and dryer. Then, when James or Anne is cleaning up renters' messes they'll be earning some pocket change!

If you choose to install coin-operated laundry equipment you should report the income you receive from the equipment.

discourage good renters and are a breeding ground for bad renters. You will have to hire someone to regularly complete property maintenance on shared rental areas. Tenants don't usually voluntarily keep shared areas clean and tidy. Good renters who do this, will quit and move out of your building if shared areas continually become messy.

If you provide laundry facilities that more than one rental unit must share, consider the possibility of purchasing and installing coin-operated equipment. If you find yourself cleaning the laundry facility at least you'll be earning some extra income. In this case, as your own property maintenance you can keep this income. But do realize you must report it money earned—just like any other rental income.

- The biggest disadvantage to renting is bad tenants. You may have heard the phrase "A bad apple will spoil the whole barrel." The same can be true with renters; if you have one bad renter and seven good renters eventually the good renters will leave your building. Only bad renters will want to live in your building. Loud parties, drugs, and other disruptive activities become commonplace.

Probably the biggest disadvantage is that multiple renters in a closely confined building may not get along. If you become a haven for bad renters, your rental property's reputation will go the same way.

What would be the advantages or disadvantages of a rental property you would consider purchasing?

Already a landlord

Congratulations!

You have the most important requirement for a landlord: land or more specifically, something over which you can lord!

Just kidding, but you do have an investment with which you can increase your financial wealth.

We're going to suggest you start by spending some time in the neighborhood surrounding the rental unit you own.

Meet the neighbors

Do you know any of the neighbors who live around your rental property? You should.

Even if you already own the property you plan to rent, or are planning to rent, meet the people who live near your rental unit because a connection with them can be vital to your successful rental property investment.

Whether or not you live near your rental, make sure your rental property neighbors have your contact information.

You want those who live near your rental property to know you care about the property. Showing that you care about the property shows respect. Hopefully they will respect you back, by calling you if they see problems or concerns.

Side Story

Eileen and Tod were searching for rental property. One afternoon they drove to a prospective property and visited with some of the neighbors. After visiting for just a few minutes they discovered the issues in the home - information not disclosed by the seller or seller's realtor and were able to negotiate a lower purchase price.

Side Story

Jane and Judy moved half way across the United States, leaving behind a lovely single-family home. They thought they might someday want to return to their home state. So they decided to rent out their former home. Jane and Judy chose a well qualified tenant. Employed at the police station where Jane had worked, their new renter came with great credentials. What they will never understand is how their tenant choice went so wrong. Their renter severely damaged the home's interior, even riding an ATV around on the roof of their beloved home!

Where were Jane and Judy's former neighbors through all of this? Oblivious, it appears, as no one bothered to call the unexpecting landlords even though Jane and Judy had left their phone number with their former neighbors. Even by providing contact information, sometimes neighbors don't care. A possible option could have been monthly calls, from Jane and Judy, to the neighbor just checking to see if everything was okay.

Protect yourself

You need insurance. Make sure your insurance company understands you're covering a rental property. If your insurance company doesn't carry policies that cover rental or investment properties, shop for another insurance company.

Consider the type of rental insurance that covers your lost rent if your home should be uninhabitable because of fire or storm damage. Costs should be reasonable, but shop around if your insurance premiums increase too quickly.

Also consider an umbrella policy. Our insurance agent has explained to us that our personal umbrella policy will provide us with extra protection - on top of our rental insurance - if an accident should occur on the property where we are held partially or fully responsible.

Cover yourself, and your assets, with insurance.

Advertise for tenants

Many options exist for landlords to advertise for clients. If the rental property is in your neighborhood, or you know people who reside nearby, consider word-of-month advertising. It's the cheapest but has a great many restrictions including no pictures available!

Local community bulletin boards may be an option. You may find them in local food markets, gas stations, or coffee houses. We've never had great results with them. You may place flyer-type ads to have someone else pull them down, deface them, or cover them with their own ads. You're stuck thinking you're advertising when your ads are gone. Be aware you'll need to check on your bulletin board ads.

Place signs in exterior areas, like yards or a window. Signs work great as advertising. We've found at least half of our applicants were simply drivebys.

We suggest every landlord needs a computer with internet access. You can use various websites to advertise for renters, but be aware that online advertising can bring a variety of renters - not always desirable tenants.

www.craigslist.com

If easily accessible, consider www.craigslist.com which is available at no additional charge (besides internet connection) both nationally and internationally.

Like we've warned, be very wary of scammers and never accept pre-payment checks. At the time First-Time Landlord went to print, each craigslist listing allows the attachment of up to four photos.

Renters in search of a new home love getting a glimpse of the house you offer. Make sure to include all costs because renters have the right to know what their expenses will be before they fill out an application.

Consider the purchase of custom-printed yard signs. Search the internet for "yard sign." We've started to use signs printed with our name, it seems to be effective, and we lose fewer signs!

Find renters

Finding renters is different from advertising for renters, because ads get to everyone – you find renters by looking for what you consider to be good renters.

Consider everyone who contacts you as a potential renter, but just because they respond to your advertising they may not be desirable tenants.

Here's where your real work starts, or you may end up evicting and removing bad renters - and that's way more work!

Choose tenants

Next we must talk about who you can and cannot choose as your tenants. Fair housing regulations state that you cannot select—or not select—your renters based on the following criteria.

Side Story

Mike/Elaine's rental properties are more than a few blocks from their home. Sometimes potential renters make appointments they later decide not to keep. Rather than calling to cancel, they'll just "forget" the appointment.

Later they may call to apologize and reschedule. Mike and Elaine keep a list of renters who have stood them up, and refuse to schedule appointments with them again unless the potential tenant has a very good excuse.

BEFORE renters

Tenant Tip

As a landlord you legally need to keep any prejudices you hold, to yourself.

Tenants have many rights, don't you - operating as a landlord - wrong them!

This means that based on these factors you cannot choose who you will, or will not, accept as renters:

- Race
- Color
- Religion
- Sex
- Handicap
- Familiar Status
- National Origin

That means you cannot reject someone based on the color of their skin, what church they attend or do not attend, and whether or not they have a handicap.

If you have a one-bedroom home obviously you do not have to rent it to a family of four. That's your right and also local regulations may dictate how many persons may occupy a bedroom. Both of our duplex properties are in the same city. The city's rental regulations stipulate no more than two people per bedroom. That means in a two-bedroom unit no more than four people can reside. Check your local laws. They may be different in various parts of the country.

You have a right to know rental applicant income and sources of additional monies. If you see that the potential tenant cannot afford your rent, you can reject them.

If you have a three-story house you are probably not required to make the entire home wheelchair accessible, but check your local regulations. You do have rights but remember when you advertise - choose your audience.

The next sections cover your first contact with new potential renters.

Since most conversations will very likely be over the phone, your verbal communication should be evaluated first.

Here goes...

Listen to applicants

Once a potential applicant starts to talk to you, be prepared to listen. Especially over the telephone, be attentive to everything your possible future tenant is saying to you.

If they brag about themselves, cringe. Remember this is what they want you to believe about them. Listen politely.

You will learn more about them from their application form, if they are interested in your rental property.

But we've turned people down, or discouraged them, right over the phone.

First, if they haven't seen photos of your rental or done a driveby, they may not realize the size or logistics of your rental property.

Listen to what they say.

Don't waste your time or theirs. Be attentive to what they need in a rental unit.

Talk to applicants

Ask a potential applicant about themselves and their family.

If you have policies on pets bring it up now. You don't want to waste anyone's time if you are not open to pets. If they have more pets than you accept, discuss it now.

Regarding pets, if a caller finds out you don't accept dogs, and they already admit they have two, be cautious if they offer to get "rid" of the pets and not move in with them.

Elaine says straight out, "We don't want renters who would get rid of their dogs." Mike says, "We don't want to separate renters from their dogs."

Mike's nicer, but we both know the renter probably won't really get rid of their dog. What they may do is bring it in when you're not around!

Side Story

Mike/Elaine have a duplex that looks like a one-level home from the street. It appears to be a small rambler, but really has three levels and an additional small home is attached on the side away from the street. People often call because they think it's a small single family home when it's a large two-family building. Each time it's vacant at least one person calls saying "I live in the neighborhood and we're looking for a house for my mother." Elaine gently explains "The house looks like a small rambler but really..." Don't be rude to someone who calls inquiring about your rental, it may not be right for them, or their mother. If you're courteous, they may pass on the description of your property to someone who is looking for just your rental!

BEFORE renters

Side Story

Mike/Elaine had a tenant, Mark who stayed four years. That sounds good, but really Mark was not a good renter. Mark had a supposedly "indoor" cat which he left outside to do his job. Mike found "deposits" on the lawn as large as those made by a dog.

Worse case: after Mark moved out Mike had to replace all the carpets. Inside a bedroom Mike found massive cat urine stains on the floor - right by the door.

It appeared the cat had been locked in the bedroom and could not alert anyone that he (the cat) needed to go outside and do his "job."

In this case it wasn't the cat's fault, it was the tenant's fault.

We do not accept dogs after some very bad experiences with a few dog owners. We're not saying the dogs were bad. The owners of the dogs were bad.

It wasn't the dog's fault. Generally dogs create messes inside homes because their owners or caregivers didn't give them enough outside breaks or are negligent in training them to do their job outside.

We do accept indoor declawed/neutered cats, but always require an additional pet damage deposit. We stipulate indoor cat. Cats who do not stay indoors—all the time—can leave deposits on your lawn as large as some left by dogs. Be specific!

Landlord Line

A quick "how many in your family" may throw off someone trying to avoid telling you that he and his three friends want to rent your one bedroom unit.

Help applicants

Whether you have a caring personality or not, providing a nice house for a family benefits tenants. Potential applicants are usually individuals or families who are in a financial or geographical situation where they cannot buy a home. Sometimes it's for monetary reasons, other times it's because they plan on living in the area only for a shorter period of time and only want a temporary home.

For some families and individuals financial problems may prevent them from currently — or ever—having the credit or cash to purchase a home.

For other families and individuals their reasons may not be so obvious:

- military career brings them temporarily to your area so they know they'll be moving again;

- job has transferred them to your area for a short period of time so purchasing a home would not be fiscally smart; and

- a move across the country has brought them to your area and they're not sure where they would want to purchase a home.

Remember, you are providing a service. Tenants have choices, make choosing your rental property seem like a good choice.

Even if you don't feel like it, act helpful. Elaine thinks you might surprise yourself and end up enjoying the experience!

Don't count on applicants

Does this sound contradictory to the last guideline? It really isn't.

If a potential applicant tells you that they want to see your vacant or soon-to-be vacant rental property don't believe they will show up.

Thinking that probably sounds pessimistic, we're merely stating after years of experience that sometimes potential tenants who make appointments to see a property don't show up at all. Maybe they found something else, or?

We keep a list, gladly a short list, of potential renters who have called, made an appointment with us and stood us up without even a call. Our closest rental unit is twenty miles from our home so when we leave our house to show a vacant, or soon to be vacant, rental unit we have miles to drive.

We understand renters can have reasons or excuses:

- a last minute emergency with their child,
- their car runs out of gas or breaks down,
- a sudden call from work changes all their plans,
- someone calls with news about a fun party out at the beach,
- or they forget.

Except for last two excuses, we will gladly accept an apology for legitimate reasons.

Tenant Tip

If a potential rental applicant schedules a unit viewing with you, make sure to request and receive a contact phone number. You may have to call and reschedule, thereby needing a phone contact. But if they decide to skip the meeting with you that gives you a form of contact. Your time is valuable, too.

Tenant Tip

If an open rental unit is vacant feel free to allow applicants to view the unit. But if a soon-to-be-former tenant still has possessions on the premises you must never ever leave an applicant alone in a room. You are legally obligated to protect your tenants possessions as long as they are your tenants.

BEFORE renters

Side Story

Mike/Elaine had received a phone call from a potential applicant who was in his car outside our empty rental property. He wanted to see it now—but we live 20 miles away.

In the phone conversation, Mike scheduled an appointment with the applicant. Mike showed up, but the potential applicant was not there. Mike called the potential applicant and he said he could not come to the property - because he was homeless!

He had not left himself enough time to find a new home!

Sometimes it happens, we understand because most everyone we know has forgotten or missed an appointment.

Sometimes potential renters don't even call back. We sometimes will call them back, so make sure you've gotten a contact phone number from them in your last conversation or email.

When we call them back, we simply remind them about the appointment they had made with us. If they are casual or flippant in their answer, we place their name on our "we won't show" list.

You have the right to decline showing a rental unit to a caller who is not considerate and doesn't at least call, or apologize, when they must miss an appointment - an appointment they chose to schedule.

Remember, you are not being paid for your time in showing rental units, but it doesn't mean your time is worth nothing!

List what you feel would make a good applicant, check back later and see if you want to add, or delete, from the list. What do you find most important in a potential applicant?

Section 8/ Public Housing Assistance

Government housing programs are a vital part of our society. Many legitimate tenants need assistance in providing for a decent home for their families.

We no longer accept applicants with public housing assistance. You should check your state to see if you have a legal right to make the same choice.

Here's our reason – we cannot start with a periodic tenancy, our preferred form of initial contract. Government housing programs, at least the ones with whom we have worked, require a year-long lease. Our problem is that locks us, and our public-aide receiving tenant, to a long-term lease. Things can go bad and neither landlord nor renter can break the contract, unless both choose to do so.

Who's paying for what

Before you place tenants in your rental property, you need to determine who is responsible for paying various utilities and services provided for the premises.

Landlords are responsible for (any) rental property mortgage, property taxes, and house insurance. Landlords should calculate the monthly rent to include those amounts so that essentially the monthly rent is reimbursing the landlord's out-of-pocket expenses.

You can expect tenants to pay for their own utilities and city services. What may not be legal in your area, and is definitely not allowed in ours - is to require a tenant to pay any portion of another tenant's utilities, unless they both share the same rental home. Basically, one renter cannot be responsible for the utilities in another rental unit.

Side Story

Christine called in desperate need. She and her four children were living out of her car. Christine had been receiving public assistance for sixteen years. Her social worker gave her high recommendations. Mike/Elaine agreed to Christine renting a single-family home they had available.

Within six months, Mike/Elaine were attempting to evict Christine within the court system. Neighbors had reported up to a dozen people living in the home, while public assistance only allowed Christine and her four children. Mike/Elaine's eviction action failed. The judge refused without giving any grounds for the denial.

In the following weeks, two felons were arrested in the home and numerous adults when stopped in the neighborhood told police that Christine's residence was their residence. Mike/Elaine passed this information to public assistance and three months later Christine was dropped from public assistance – after nearly two decades of receiving government help.

Mike/Elaine were left with over $9,000 in property damage.

BEFORE renters

BEFORE renters

Tenant Tip

Mike/Elaine have found tenants really appreciate the utility incentive program. It enables them to control their costs, while you as landlord still ensure that your utility bills are being paid—because you are paying the utility statements!

Where you have more than one rental unit sharing the same meter or service connection, you should pay the utility bills, but hold the tenants responsible. Renters, just like homeowners, should be more careful of their utility use if they are paying for the utilities themselves. We help them by giving them a reward: their money back.

Utility Incentive

We require renters - who share utilities with another rental unit - to submit, as part of their monthly rent, a pre-determined amount of money that should cover their current utilities. We pre-calculate what the utilities should be (sometimes just a guesstimate because utility costs can change suddenly) and we pre-charge tenants for utilities by adding the amount to the monthly rental. Warning: you should advertise the unit rent including this amount. Tenants have a right to know what their monthly rent will be, so you must calculate this amount before advertising your unit.

If your rental units sharing a utility are the same size (each 1,000 square feet) simply divide the utility cost in half. If units are not the same size, divide them by the square footage. If one unit is 1500 square feet and the other is 950 square feet, you could possibly divide it by the square footage. Using the number of bedrooms in each unit as another way to calculate utility use.

We choose to call this a utility incentive, because if their actual use is lower than the amount they've submitted (with their monthly rent) then we give them money back. If their actual use is higher than the amount they've submitted (with their monthly rent) we expect them to reimburse us. In our lease, we state that if our contract is ended with the tenant moving out, then we will hold a portion of their security/damage deposit until the final utility bills (covering the period of time they were in the rental unit) have been received. If they have overpaid, we give them the money back in a check. Try not to just reduce their rent when reimbursing them. Reducing rent can be confusing to the tenant. Repayment in the form of a check from you, is preferable to cash. Cash payments cannot be tracked as easily.

With month-to-month/periodic rentals, we try to recalculate shared utilities every three months. In a definite length/longer term rental we just wait until the end of the contract period or if the utility cost has skyrocketed we require the excess utilities to be submitted if the amount owed is more than half their security/damage deposit. Don't let this get out of hand, but when utilities are shared by more than one rental unit we've found this to be a fair approach.

Deposit for security/damage

Don't allow a tenant to place even a cardboard box in your rental property without providing you with a complete security/damage deposit and signing a written lease.

What is a security/damage deposit? It is a sum of money, determined by the landlord, but usually similar to a month's rent on the property. For instance, if rent is $1,000 another $1,000 should be submitted for security/damage deposit.

Some suggest that making the security/damage deposit exactly the same as a month's rent is confusing to renters. They think that they can substitute the security/damage deposit for their last month's rent. Make your own choice. If tenants don't want to pay their rent, they won't. Keep it simple for yourself; requiring the same amount for monthly rent as security/damage deposit is easy to remember.

Verbally tell a potential renter what security/damage deposit is required. Tell them they must submit security/damage deposit at the time of lease signing. When you meet to sign the lease, accept the security/damage deposit before you sign the lease. Never sign a lease without receiving a security/damage deposit.

Explain that if applicants decide not to move in – after lease has been signed – you will hold the security/damage deposit. It is your right. Why?

BEFORE renters

After a lease has been signed you can no longer show your property to any other potential renter. You have made a commitment to your new renter. In return, they have made a commitment.

In at least some states, renters cannot choose to use their security deposit as their last month's rent, but placing it in your lease is also a good idea.

Security/damage deposit is insurance that the new renter will be responsible for the property while in their possession, take care of it, and if they or anyone they allow in their home should cause damage this amount is held for any repair necessary.

Like all legal concerns, make sure you receive legal counsel and check with your state about legal regulations.

Talk renters insurance

Renters insurance is vital. Like all other suggestions we've given, seek legal advice to make your own choices.

Our insurance agent is vital to our rental property business. We trust him very much and we won't share his name for two reasons: his client list is limited to residents of our state and he's so good we don't want him to get so busy he doesn't have time for us as his clients!

But we share his name with our tenants. Our insurance agent, let's call him Chris, has told us we can require our tenants to carry renters insurance. Place a clause, requiring renters insurance and insist your tenants show you their insurance policy whenever you renew their lease. Your renters should require their renter's insurance policy to list you as "Additional insureds under their liability portion of their insurance." Add to your contract that they should give you proof of this – it will be a piece of paper stating that you are listed as an additional insured.

Side Story

Mike/Elaine had owned their first duplex for less than four months when a fire broke out within both units.

Neither of their tenants had rental insurance. Mike/Elaine's insurance service providers, in the fire cleanup, were not allowed to even touch the tenants' property because it was not covered by insurance.

If you have a fire or insurance covered damage and your renters' possessions are present, it is always better that your tenants have renters insurance.

Without it, your insurance provider's recovery/reconstruction services cannot even physically touch your tenants' belongings. What a mess!

Even if different insurance companies are involved, all will cooperate in an insurance cleanup if all involved are protected by insurance.

Submit last month's rent

Requiring a somewhat financially shaky tenant to submit an extra month's rent, their last month's rent, is another form of insurance: for you as their landlord.

Tough to require, but this could save your landlord/tenant relationship with a renter who would otherwise have been refused. Explain that to them.

Landlord Line

Say, "Submitting your last month's rent now, can be a good deal for you." Faced with requiring a last month's rent submission for a financially troubled past potential renter, explain that in the long run it can be a very good deal for your applicant. Say their current rent is $1,375. If they continue to sign new leases with you their rent in five years could have risen up to a higher level. Let's choose $1,500. Don't mention the higher level in a dollar amount to your renter, right now. You could scare them away and you really don't know what amount you can charge for rent in the future.

Anyway, let's get back to your renter. In those five years your previously troubled tenant has saved money and is ready to buy their own home.

As they're getting ready to close on their house they don't have to submit their last month's rent—because they did it five years ago. And by depositing their last month's rent five years earlier they saved themselves $125 off their last month's rent!

Side Story

Mike/Elaine have faced troubled renters with many problems in their past, so they were prepared when Sally and Payne turned in their completed applications. As a condition to Sally and Payne's rental, Mike/Elaine required a last month's rent payment. Not surprisingly, Sally and Payne had trouble making this extra month's payment. But it happened. Then just a few weeks later they stopped paying the rent. Sally and Payne's excuse: "We're trying to get ahead." Mike/Elaine filed for eviction, always a tough action to take, but they felt better going into court knowing that Sally and Payne had already pre-submitted their last month's rent.

BEFORE renters

Part 1 : BEFORE renters

Have you covered all these topics? If not, review this list until you are comfortable with your decisions. Are you ready to be a landlord?

- ❏ Getting started
- ❏ Property maintenance
- ❏ Property management
- ❏ Tax advantages
- ❏ Good stuff
- ❏ Not so good stuff
- ❏ Think about becoming a landlord
- ❏ Intimidation
- ❏ Feel like a landlord
- ❏ Landlord partners
- ❏ Choose a rental property
- ❏ Pay for a rental property
- ❏ Single family, duplex, or multi-unit
- ❏ Already a landlord

- ❏ Meet the neighbors
- ❏ Protect yourself
- ❏ Advertise for tenants
- ❏ Find renters
- ❏ Choose tenants
- ❏ Listen to applicants
- ❏ Talk to applicants
- ❏ Help applicants
- ❏ Don't count on applicants
- ❏ Section 8/Public Housing Assistance
- ❏ Who's paying for what
- ❏ Deposit for security/damage
- ❏ Talk renters insurance
- ❏ Submit last month's rent

BEFORE
renters

BEFORE renters

BEFORE renters

BEFORE
renters

BEFORE renters

BEFORE renters

Part 2
DURING renters

New renters

How you initially deal with renters as they move in is a big deal. Whether your new renter only stays a few months, or fifteen years, your first communications can reflect on all future communications.

Elaine likes to come across friendly. Mike likes to come across gruff. Just ask their tenants!

Refer to Landlord Partners, to review some suggestions on appearing united to your tenants, and when it's okay to be "good landlord/bad landlord."

Friendly not friends

A term that's been around for a long time, it means what it says. Be on good terms with your renters, but do not socialize with them on a regular basis. Your friends expect special treatment, including favors, from you. Your tenants should not.

Starting your relationship on a professional, but friendly, level gives tenants the understanding that they can talk to you about house issues that concern them. That's what matters.

Don't deceive renters into thinking they will automatically become best of friends with you.

Side Story

Kevin and Nancy signed a lease to rent a home from Larry. Larry was very friendly and told Kevin and Nancy that he wanted to come over for barbecues and to spend time together. Contrary to what Larry first said, he ended up stalking Kevin and Nancy, by walking up and down their deck and yelling at them to turn off their lights. Eventually Kevin and Nancy left without giving a notice because they couldn't take Larry constantly standing in the yard they were renting, staring at the rental house. Friends? No way!

Application process

Potential renters start the application process in their first phone or email conversation with you. Are they attentive, quick to answer your questions, and willing to listen?

Elaine was talking to a potential renter who repeatedly couldn't keep track of the conversation. To Elaine that didn't mean he was not interested, it's more likely he is anxious. Just a warning flag, it doesn't mean this could not be a good renter. Don't make your decisions too early, you could be wrong.

If they brag what great renters they are, please try not to believe them. If they apply for your rental, check all their credentials and that will give you a better insight into their credibility as great renters.

What you want to listen to is how they speak to you about: themselves, their jobs, their interests and hobbies.

Always require potential renters to look at your rental unit before filling out an application form. Would you want to live somewhere without seeing it first? Logically, a renter searching for a new home would feel the same way. If they want to fill out an application without seeing the rental property just say "no." That means they are desperate and don't want to share that with you, or they don't care about where they live and that's probably just as bad.

Give application forms to everyone you'd like, treat them like they're candy. But remind everyone that the first completed and returned form will mean you will not accept another application unless the applicant is rejected or refuses to sign a lease. Your property is not legally rented unless you have a lease.

Accept no application form without an application fee. We did that too many times when we first become landlords. Because we had no fee involved, applicants would fill out and give us an application form, then continue looking for another rental unit. We gave them no incentive to stop and question if our rental unit was the perfect one for them.

We find requiring $100, per applicant, weeds out applicants who are just shopping. We use a portion of the amount to pay for a credit check and return the remainder of the $100 to them, in the form of reduced second month's rent, if they are accepted. If the applicant simply changes their mind we return nothing to them.

Whether or not you continue to show your available rental unit, when you are processing an application, should be your personal choice. But you need to be honest.

Here are the options we consider:

- If the rental unit is currently occupied with a tenant who is still under lease with you, we would no longer show the rental unit. It would be disrespectful to inconvenience a current renter with more showings.

- If your rental unit is vacant, with no occupant, then we would consider showing it to additional potential renters. You must notify all new potential renters though, that you are already processing an application.

It doesn't hurt to have a backup plan in case an applicant decides to rent elsewhere, or fails your credit and reference checks.

Application Form

We want to jump the gun a bit. We'll talk about filling out the applications but first we need to talk about how to view your renters. Unless you own a house and are renting out rooms of your house to other people (which by the way may be the only time to break the no friends or family policy because who really wants to live with strangers) look at applicants who want to share one rental unit as a group.

That means, if you are renting out your house and three friends want to live together, they must all fill out applications, if they are adults.

We'll explain more later, but you want all adults to be equally responsible for a home they are renting from you.

If individuals are leasing a unit together they should have one lease. That way, if one friend gets mad at the others they cannot walk out and leave the other two paying you their share of the rent. That's because you will end up with less rent, fewer renters, and more problems! We'll talk more about this under **Lease.**

Now, back to application forms.

We suggest you seek legal support in creating any documents you utilize with potential, present, or past renters. We offer samples of document information we use only as suggestions and do not make a legal commitment that they are most appropriate for your use. Make your own choice and seek legal assistance whenever appropriate.

Following are the components we find necessary for an application form. Both social security number and birth date of each applicant are absolutely necessary to complete a credit check. Each adult applicant must fill out a separate form. You can build your form so that a married couple could both complete the same form. Or you could require married applicants to complete separate forms.

Some suggest including a great deal of non-relevant information on an application form. We know applicants may be filling out forms at other rental properties and have a life, so we only ask for what is required to complete a credit and reference check.

Components of an application form:

1. Start with a title which includes your business name or your personal name. Consider adding your phone number. If potential applicants depart without giving you the completed application form, then having your phone number on the form is handy. You may think of an application form as an advertisement. The applicant then knows where and how to contact you.

2. Title should also include the title of your application form. We suggest this title: Residential Rental Occupancy Application. That way there's no misunderstanding exactly what your rental property includes.

3. Next leave plenty of space for full legal name and require applicants print out their entire legal name. Spell it out for them. You don't want nicknames.

4. Add a space for a telephone number, maybe include space for a second phone number if you like.

5. Continue with social security number.

6. Don't forget the birth date of applicant (including year of course) as this is vital to a credit check. Credit checks quickly determine if applicant is legitimate because social security number and birth date have a matching code. They can tell, and it's cool.

7. Repeat 3. through 6. We've found with today's active adults that each applicant, even if they're married, usually has a separate telephone number.

8. Next include current or present address. If they're living with extended family that would be their address. Also ask for past addresses, especially if they have not lived long at their present address.

9. List city, state, and zip code of each address, current, and past.

10. Include how many in the family. Remember they are making a commitment to you regarding the number of people in their family.

11. Give them space to write how long they have been at their present address.

Side Story

Elaine was showing a duplex to Tom and Toni. They both appeared quiet but they also both worked night shifts and it was 10:00 in the morning so Elaine concluded they were probably tired. With twin toddlers in their van, Tom and Toni took turns looking at the rental home. Toni and Tom briefly discussed the home and told Elaine they wanted to immediately fill out an application.

Elaine waited while they did this. Tom and Toni listed they had four children. Later, when Elaine was calling Tom and Toni's personal references, a family member stated that they had five children. Elaine knew this was a red flag because she had mentioned to Tom and Toni that the city rental regulations only allowed two persons per bedroom. The duplex is a three-bedroom home so deception had occurred on the application form. Though Elaine regretted having to decline Tom and Toni, she found another excuse. Later Tom called and left a message apologizing for the lie about their family size. Elaine still wishes Mike/Elaine could have rented to Tom and Toni, but other issues may have come up. It's best to check references thoroughly.

DURING renters

12. Require their present landlord's name and telephone number.

13. Follow that with their prior landlord's name and telephone number.

14. Next make a bolder title for their work references.

15. Require company name, applicant's position or job title at company, and how long they've been employed at the firm.

16. Add space for their supervisor or a contact person at the firm, and telephone number for that person.

17. Conclude the work references section with their salary - it's definitely legal for you to ask because you have a right to know if they can afford to pay the monthly rent you currently require.

18. Add a space for additional income and request the source of income: disability, spousal or child support, or a trust fund?

19. Repeat 15. through 18. for their spouse, if they are married and you don't require a separate form for spouse. As we've mentioned, we don't require a separate form for a married spouse.

20. Add a title for personal references. Include lines for three personal references including name, relationship, and telephone number.

21. Add one last title for professional references. Include lines for name, professional relationship, and telephone number.

22. Conclude with the following text, with which they will be making a commitment: "I represent that the information provided in this application is true to the best of my knowledge. You are hereby authorized to verify my credit and employment references in connection with the processing of this application. I understand that I must pay a $100 (author's note: that's

what we require) fee to apply for rental. If I am approved I will receive a $70 (or whatever amount is left after credit check) discount on my second months's rent. $30 (author's note: or whatever amount is required for credit check) is not refundable as it is an expense for a third-party credit check. If I wish to withdraw as an applicant any remaining amount of $100 application fee will not be returned to me. If I am not approved as a result of the credit check, Wencl/Creative, Inc (author's note: place your name or business name here) will refer me to the firm providing the credit check so they can forward the appropriate information for my use. All credit checks are confidential and Wencl/Creative, Inc. (author's note: again place your name or business name here) will not share this information with any non-business related parties."

23. Finally add a line for date application was completed and signature or signatures of applicants.

24. Optional choice would be to include an Equal Opportunity Housing logo. We have not done so to this time - we practice it though and believe everyone has the same rights. If you are unfamiliar with the logo just search for it on the internet under "equal opportunity housing." Housing discrimination is illegal. Discuss with a legal professional if you'd like more information.

Credit Check

A credit check provides verification of an applicant's work, credit, criminal, fraud, and housing records. You cannot complete a credit check on your own. Trust us, we've tried. Our recommendation is to go with an online service which pays fees to be able to search multiple records.

Complete a credit check first, before you start a reference check. If their credit is not what

Tenant Tip

When you, as landlord, call for references and follow up on information provided on an application form, we suggest you make notes on the front and back of the original form. Make sure to use a different color pen so your notes differ in appearance from the applicant information.

We talked to other landlords who say you should never make notes on the application form. They say you should duplicate the application form and make your notes on a separate copy. We believe it adds to the authenticity of the credit check to use the same form.

A third option would be to simply make notes on a separate sheet and attach it to the original form.

The choice is up to you—the landlord! Once again, seek legal counsel whenever you have questions.

you find acceptable, you will have avoided a possible embarrassment for the applicant.

Choose a reliable firm to complete your credit check. You may choose to join a credit bureau, but we have found very satisfactory results by using a national-level firm who serve both the employment and rental industry.

Other firms serve the field, but we have been very happy with RHR Information Services, Inc. at http://www.rhris.com.

We checked with RHR Information Services before listing them in *First-Time Landlord* as a credit check reference. We receive no financial or beneficial kickback for recommending RHR. We've just been very pleased with RHR.

Charging a nominal fee, RHR provides an online credit check in one to four days, depending on the applicant. *First-Time Landlord*, when going to press, pays $30 for a one-time application credit check. Never give a potential applicant a paper copy, or show them their results online, of their credit check. It is not legal. What's great about RHR is that they will offer the applicant a copy of their completed credit check – just tell your applicant to contact RHR. That's why we recommend RHR: they're easy to access and will provide your applicant with a copy of the completed credit check.

We feel totally comfortable requiring our applicants to pay for their own credit checks, because they can receive a copy of the credit check.

Reference Check

On our application form we ask our applicants to list normal things like their current and last employment, housing, and income. We also ask them to list three personal and three professional references.

We've gained the most information from the personal and professional reference checks.

Put it in writing

That's the lease. Think of it as your rules book since the lease you and your renter or renters share controls your relationship. Never rent without a written contract/lease.

If you purchase a rental property with existing renters not covered by a written contract, require them to sign a printed lease as soon as possible. If no written contract exists, many states treat a tenancy as if it is a periodic, or month-to-month agreement.

If renters are currently renting in a property you just purchased, you should talk to the seller before closing the deal. Actually, you may not even want to make an offer if you can't see the leases. Check over the lease or leases. Speak to the current renters and ask to see their lease. Expect lies, because that's what might happen to you. It happened to us.

Periodic tenancy/Month-to-month

We suggest starting all renters on a periodic tenancy which means their contract runs month-to-month. A periodic tenancy does not require an ending date so a contract like this could cover a rental agreement for many years. Month-to-month leases also allow you to get to know your tenant without a long-term commitment. Unless either the landlord or tenant requests a change in the lease, you may want to keep it a month-to-month rental.

Check with your state, it will vary but on a periodic lease the landlord is able to more easily adjust the rent because of changing circumstances. In our state, a landlord must deliver written notice to a current tenant, at least one month and one day before the new lease is to take effect.

Warning; if your rental is somewhere with significant climate changes, you may not fare as well if your renter decides to leave in the middle of winter (in snow country) or the middle of summer (in desert country.) It will be harder to find new renters.

Side Story

Mike/Elaine purchased their first rental property from the Simpsons. They seemed like a nice couple - hah! They'd actually switched contracts on their renters: Randy and Sue. Simpsons had updated their contract when a friend moved in by changing the end of the contract to a longer period of time, on their (the Simpsons) version of the lease. You might not have caught what they did, Mike/Elaine sure didn't. For a better sale price on their rental property, Simpsons changed the lease on Randy and Sue - so it looked like they were going to stay longer.

Really, people would do that! Now Mike/Elaine know better and if they were to buy a home with current renters they'd spend way more time with the renters. By the way, Simpsons also told Randy and Sue, when Mike/Elaine walked through the home before making an offer - to tell Mike/Elaine that all the appliances worked - even though they didn't!

That's where the value of definite-term leases come in handy. Yes, you as landlord have made a commitment not to change the rent but your tenant has also made a commitment not to leave.

Definite-Term tenancy

Terms that cover a specific period of time and include an ending date are called definite-term leases. The length of the lease has been determined.

Generally, if a definite-term lease goes beyond its "expiration" date and no new lease has been signed with the current tenant it may legally change into a periodic or month-to-month lease.

If you choose, you can have a buyout clause, where a tenant can leave for certain reasons like purchasing a home or a legitimate job transfer to an area more than one hour's drive from the rental location.

We don't offer a buyout clause and you probably don't have to - that's a legal issue. If you offer a buyout clause a fair amount might be two months of rent. If rent is $1,000 per month, then you'd be asking for $2,000 and they can walk away from their rental obligation.

Definite-term leases can be most any length. Our shortest-term lease was three months. Our potential renters were building a new home and had sold their former home. They needed a place quick. Though they would only reside in our rental home for just over two months they submitted three months of rent to make sure they could stay longer if needed.

The longest definite-term leases we have offered are two years in length. You may not choose to do that, but we were comfortable with our renters and felt just as comfortable knowing they had made a two year commitment to us.

Lease

A lease is a legally binding commitment between landlord and tenant. In our contracts we refer to ourselves in our role as landlord/property manager with the title: Lessor. Our tenants/renters we refer to as: Lessee. Rental contracts consist of two roles: Lessor - landlord who is offering a property for lease purposes; and Lessee who is agreeing to a contractual agreement allowing and limiting their use of the rental property.

Leases are definitely the most complicated part of any rental agreement. Within a written contract you are stipulating how you, as landlord, and your renter, as tenant, are to act during and at the end of your lease period.

Before we go forward let's talk, as we've mentioned before, about who should be on the lease. All adults residing in a single rental unit should be on one lease, with each of them as the lessees and you as the lessor.

Also as we've mentioned elsewhere, if you reside in the home where you are renting out individual rooms and you are sharing some rooms in common, you almost surely would want separate leases with each renter. They are renting specific separate areas of the rental property so logically their leases should be separate.

But just last evening, Elaine was talking on the phone with a potential renter who wanted to divide the living space of the rental unit in half.

Let's call her Kim. Kim would be responsible for one half of the rent, and her friend, let's call her Beth, would be responsible to us for the other half. Elaine explained how this couldn't work, because if Beth wanted to leave and end the lease, but Kim wanted to stay - then Mike/Elaine would be stuck. We would either have to ask Kim to leave or find another friend to move in. Or just accept half the rent for the unit.

Nope, it's better for everyone involved if all adult tenants are on the lease. Legally, at least in our state, there's an advantage for the landlord. If all renters move out without proper notice, owing rent, and leave damage - then the landlord is only required to sue one of the tenants. A landlord does not have to locate each of the renters, at least in our state. One tenant can be sued for all the damage. It may sound unfair to the tenant who is stuck with all the costs, but that tenant can then turn around and sue their other former co-tenants. (See page 68 for "Change the Lease.")

Landlord Line

Remember, unless you are renting a share of the house you call home, you can definitely require all adult tenants to be on the same lease. It's to your benefit for many reasons including the fact that you would only have to sue one tenant. Each tenant is responsible for 100% of the rent.

Take the time

Submit your lease to your potential renter before they take possession of the premises. Sit with them, if you must, and read through each clause. Require them to read the entire contract before they sign. In our state a rental lease is legally binding as soon as it is signed. No three-day-waiting period here, as soon as it is signed it is a contract. Verbally remind new renters of this. If your renter is signing a new contract, continuing from another lease agreement with you, offer them the contract earlier and give them a few days to read it.

Do not allow a potential renter to leave with an unsigned contract, or a contract only you have signed. You don't know what they will do with the contract.

Do you feel you tend to rush into things sometimes? Don't do it now. As a landlord you should feel obligated to make sure your new applicant understands the terms of the lease that will govern both of you: landlord and tenant. Are you ready?

Listed are some of the clauses you may want to include in your leases:

- **Periodic Tenancy.** Our suggestion is to start a new renter with periodic tenancy which is a month-to-month rental that requires either party (landlord or renter) to give at least one month and one day written notice before the contract can be changed or dissolved. By starting with a periodic tenancy a short-term commitment provides an opportunity to see if landlord and tenant are a good match.

- **Definite-Term Tenancy.** If by your past experience with a new renter you feel comfortable with a new tenant, offer a definite-term lease. Or if a period tenancy renter pays the rent on time and takes good care of your house, offer them a definite-term lease. As a landlord a definite-term lease means a renter has agreed to pay a fixed sum of money each month in rent.

  You as landlord, should benefit by receiving a longer commitment from the renter.

  The tenant benefits with the reassurance that their rent will remain stable for a set length of time. In cooler weather, northern climates find fewer renters looking to move in winter months which makes a definite-term lease ending in summer months a more attractive alternative. Generally, tenants don't want to move in very cold, or very hot weather.

- **Application Fee.** Charge an application fee when prospective renters want to rent a unit you have available. Though some property management firms encourage this, don't accept an application fee if you have no unit open. That's not fair and not nice. By requiring an application fee potential tenants are making a monetary commitment.

  We suggest deducting the cost of the credit check from the application fee. Potential renters realize you are serious about

Side Story

Eric signed a month-to-month lease, renting a single-family home from Steve.

Steve lived about an hour away from his rental home. The second month Eric's rent check never arrived at Steve's home. Eric replaced the check but it bounced. Yes, Eric replaced it, but now it was the middle of the month.

Eric never offered any explanation. The next month Eric's rent check bounced again, with the same pattern repeating.

Steve decided it was better to dissolve the lease, so Steve mailed and delivered an end-of-lease notice to Eric. It is simpler to end a month-to-month lease because it only takes a month and one day to remove what could have become a troublesome tenant.

Side Story

Elaine had met with Sharon who had a good job history and was anxious to move to a new home. Sharon had been divorced several years earlier and her ex-husband had been legally obligated to take on business debt. During Sharon's credit check Elaine discovered that Sharon's ex-husband had not removed the debt from Sharon's record—in fact Sharon owed a great deal of money because of her ex-husband's business debt. Sharon was upset to hear that her credit report listed her as a debtor but she thanked Elaine for sharing the information.

Tenant Tip

It is not a tenant choice if their security/damage deposit is used for their last month's rent. Some landlords recommend requiring a security/damage deposit that is a different amount than the monthly rent, so tenants won't auotmically assume their security deposit will cover their last month's rent.

checking them out and some will decline just because they know what you will find. Others welcome the opportunity to receive an up-to-date credit report.

- **Security/Damage Deposit.** Require payment of a security/damage deposit before new renters put any of their items inside your rental unit.

When a contract terminates, you will be required to return unused security/damage deposit to your former renter, or document why you did not return any sum of money.

Some states give you a deadline of a few weeks in which you must notify your former renter, in writing, about their security/damage deposit. An amount of interest, as little as 1% must also be reimbursed to your former renter on any returned sum of money. Check with your state regarding this amount of money.

As we have mentioned elsewhere, you could add to your security/damage deposit clause covering if the new renter breaks the lease by not moving into the premises. You could stipulate that the landlord will keep the security/damage deposit – because they broke the lease before move-in date. It helps ensure your new renters won't change their mind and without any loss to them refuse to take possession of your rental unit. You, as landlord, have made a commitment. Your new renter should too.

- **Last Month's Rent.** After a credit check, let's say you have found an applicant has had an eviction or a UD – an Unlawful Detainer. That means they left a former rental unit owing money to the landlord or property management. That's bad.
You don't want a tenant who will leave your rental unit owing you rent. Although their intentions are good, renters who have done this before are more likely to do it again. Carefully read the credit check. If it states

they resolved the eviction or UD, you can discuss with the applicant how it was resolved. Listen carefully. Remember you are only hearing their version. We still suggest requiring a last month's rent deposit.

Even if they haven't resolved the eviction you can accept them. But absolutely require the last month's rent submission. It is your only safeguard.

Although it's challenging for new tenants to come up with a last month's rent, remind them they created this problem. You need insurance they will not leave you, too, owing rent.

Last month's rent may seem like a hardship to your potential tenant but you have a legal right to protect your investment.

- **Pet Security/Damage Deposit.** We love pets and take care of ours. But too many tenants don't take care of their pets. Require additional damage deposit and remember, if returned you will need to add current interest, just as you would in a normal security/damage deposit.

- **Late Payments.** Late payments must be required and enforced, just like any other clause. We suggest a progressive schedule of late payments, so perpetually late payment tenants can see the value of paying their rent on time.

If you prefer receiving rental payments by USPS (United States Postal Service) we suggest the following schedule we include in our current lease: Rent payment will not incur a late fee because of late delivery by the United States Postal Service if the following procedure is followed. See end of clause for duplicate check schedule.

Side Story

Sue and Sam wanted to rent Gerry's lovely single-family rental home overlooking a river. Credit checks revealed an eviction in Sue's past and some disturbing legal problems for Sam, so Gerry required a last month's rent. After trouble making rent payments, Gerry gave Sue and Sam written notice that their month-to-month lease would be ending. Gerry was not evicting Sue and Sam, he was simply going to end their lease.

Sue and Sam protested, and the last month's rent submission Gerry had required made their last month as landlord/tenant so simple.

Side Story

While shopping for a rental property, Mike/Elaine visited a lovely side-by-side investment home. A current renter, seemed like a nice guy but he had a large dog that had physically torn a large hole in an interior door. The renter said he was going to pay for the door, but we're sure there was more damage. Yes, we did not buy that investment property.

DURING renters

If payment is later received and postmark is no later than three days prior to the last day of the month, it will not incur a late fee even if the United States Postal Service delivers it later than the first day of the month in which it is due. The examples we use follow:

In a month with 31 days (January, March, May, July, August, October, December) it would need to be postmarked before the 29th day of the month.

In a month with 30 days (April, June, September, November) it would need to be mailed before the 28th day of the month.

In a month with 28 or 29 days (February) it would need to be mailed before the 26th or 27th day of the month.

Payments can be mailed later than this schedule, but if the United States Postal Service delivers it later than the first day of the month it is due, a late fee will be incurred. In the event of late payment of any rental installment, the Lessee shall have one day to pay the full rent plus a late charge (as specified below). Rent payment more than one day late shall be considered in breach of contract. For each contract, the following late payment schedule guidelines will be enforced. First month payment one day late, a late charge of $25.00 will be incurred; second month a late charge of $50.00 will be incurred; third month a late charge of $75.00 will be incurred; fourth month a late charge of $100.00 will be incurred; fifth month a late charge of $125.00 will be incurred; sixth month a late charge of $150.00 will be incurred. After the sixth late payment, automatic eviction will occur.

Duplicate check schedule: If Lessor has not received Lessee's check by end of second day in month (July 2, August 2), Lessee must provide Lessor with a duplicate check, including late fee. When/if original check arrives at Lessor's address, check will immediately be returned to Lessee.

If United States Postal Service postmark shows it was mailed according to the described schedule (mailed no later than the third last day of the month before it was due: ex. mailed April 28 for a May rent payment) then late fee will be reimbursed to Lessee in the form of a check, by Lessor.

Insufficient/Redeposited Check by Lessee. If Lessee submits a rent payment check with insufficient funds, or check has to be resubmitted by Lessor's bank, then Lessee is responsible for all Lessor bank fees – as they relate to the Lessee's non-payment. Lessor must provide Lessee with copies of bank fees showing charges.

- **Responsible Party.** Here you list how many adults may reside at your rental unit and stipulate that they carry responsibility for actions and activities of everyone within the home – visitor or resident.

- **Appliances Provided and Their Care.** Explain what appliances you are providing at the residence and remind your renters that all appliances are for their own personal use.

    Stipulate in your lease that you are not responsible if an appliance breaks and the renter suffers a loss of perishable goods. No one is going to reimburse you if your freezer breaks and your hamburger goes bad. If you don't get reimbursed, neither should your renters.

    If you have an extra freezer in the house, which may have been sold with the house when you purchased the property you don't have to automatically replace it if it breaks. Add a clause regarding this to your lease.

- **Smoking Policy.** If you have smoking restrictions: exterior areas only or not at all, include a restriction regarding smoking in your lease.

- **Quiet Enjoyment.** We like this clause where we state the tenant must reside quietly and peacefully. Including quiet enjoyment has

Tenant Tip

Remind tenants which appliances are covered, you will replace. Appliances you provide should include the basics: refrigerator and stove/range. If you have a chest freezer in the unit, tenants will expect you will replace the freezer if it breaks. Be clear what you will replace.

Side Story

Butch and Cary called Mike/Elaine and explained that, according to them; a bird had flown into their patio door and broken the outside glass. When Mike arrived the interior pane, of the double-paned glass, was still intact, but Butch and Cary had already swept up every bit of glass from the broken window. Gone also was the bird they claimed had hit the glass. Butch and Cary were not the cleanest tenants, so Mike/Elaine were suspicious when their renters had completely removed the broken glass. But they all agreed it was "unexplained" so tenants and landlords split the cost of replacement 50/50.

allowed us to approach tenants and discuss noisy parties or disruptive activities.

- **Use of Premises.** A landlord may expect tenants would only live at a residence. But adding a clause stating the property is only private single family residence has helped us to challenge renters when we find them operating a business from the property. Trust us, someone will and you'll be happy for this lease clause.

- **Unexplained Damage to Residence.** If a tenant claims a window just suddenly broke, adding a clause covering unexplained damage allows you to require a renter to help in the repair of suspicious looking damage. We demand they pay half the cost: 50/50.

- **Number of Occupants.** Limit the number of residents by listing how many adults and how many minors/children under the age of 18 may reside within your rental unit. Two of our duplexes are within a city that states only two people may reside in each bedroom. If you have a two-bedroom house, that would mean four people including adults and children may occupy the house.

  Be firm, it's your right to limit the number of residents. Extra, undisclosed occupants will cause more wear and tear on your house.

- **Condition of Premises.** Require new tenants to examine the home and agree it is in good order, repair, clean, safe, and in tenantable condition. With this clause, you are limiting the chance a renter can claim the house was not in good condition.

- **Assignment and Subletting.** Adding a clause stating they cannot, without written permission by you, allow others to reside or replace them in your rental property gives you legal rights if you should find others living in the home.

- **Alterations and Improvements.** Clearly state that renters cannot change their rental property with permanent alterations to the rental property. A renter may suffer a disability that places them in a wheelchair. Although you might definitely want to provide wheelchair access, do not allow renter to permanently alter the rental home. Their alteration may not be up to code or may damage your property.

- **Damage to Premises.** Basically you need a clause requiring them to take blame if they damage your premises.

- **Dangerous Materials.** Add a clause stating they cannot use illegal, explosive, or otherwise dangerous materials anywhere on the rental property.

- **Utilities.** Remind renters which utilities they are required to pay. Included in utilities could be gas, electric, water, septic or sewer, and city specific utilities like trash, street lights and street water runoff. Utilities not covered by landlords usually include telephone and television satellite or cable. We suggest only accepting cable, not satellite. Satellite providers claim they will not cause roof damage or will install a ground-based dish, but in either case they leave behind hardware equipment.

- **Right of Inspection.** You have the right to inspect your rental property. Legally you should give a twenty-four hour verbal notice, but that doesn't help if you suspect illegal activities or violations of your contract like disallowed pets or additional tenants who can leave if the tenant on your lease expects you to arrive for a scheduled inspection.

If you expect breaches of your contract are occurring you need to address it as soon as you become aware of the activity—or even strongly suspect it. Hopefully a sincere discussion with your tenant will allow them to understand they need to change their actions and respect your lease.

Side Story

Kristy wanted satellite television and she wanted it bad. She didn't care that her lease with her landlord George, stated the landlord must be present for satellite or cable television installation. The local satellite provider did not notify George, the home owner, and installed a new roof-top satellite dish, right next to an older dish provided by another carrier. George protested when he saw the dish on the rental property roof, but the harm was done. When Kristy moved out a few months later, George tried to have the satellite dish providers remove their equipment. The dishes were never removed.

- **Display of Signs.** Explain that within the last thirty days of the rental lease, if a new agreement has not been signed, you have the right to display rental signs in the exterior areas of the rental property.

- **Subordination of Lease.** There's no better way to say this than the words we use: This lease and Lessee's leasehold interest hereunder are and shall be subject, subordinate, and inferior to any liens or encumbrances now or hereafter placed on the demised premises by Lessor, all advances made under any such liens or encumbrances, the interest payable on any such liens or encumbrances, and any and all renewals or extensions of such liens or encumbrances.

- **Holdover by Lessee.** Basically state that the tenant is no longer allowed to occupy the rental property when their lease has expired and not been renewed. No renter without a lease should be allowed to holdover or continue to occupy your rental property.

- **Surrender of Premises.** We'll use the words we place in our contracts: At the expiration of the lease term, Lessee shall quit and surrender the premises hereby demised in as good state and condition as they were at the commencement of this lease, reasonable use and wear thereof and damages by the elements excepted.

- **Default.** By now it may sound like we encourage a landlord to repeat, as many ways as possible, the conditions of your rental lease. That's true. In fact, we include a clause stating that if they default in their lease – they are breaching the lease. Make it clear and you can hopefully avoid legal issues.

- **Abandonment.** Here you cover your legal requirements if renters should leave behind their wanted or unwanted possessions. Unwanted possessions are what they might have considered trash, but once they are gone they may decide they are valuables and sue you for the return of them. Stating that you have the right to dispose of anything they've abandoned, or left, at your rental property may legally protect you. But store the abandoned materials and in writing try to contact them – at least it may protect you if they decide to sue.

- **Smoke Detectors.** Based on your local laws, you should have smoke detectors in all your rental properties. In between renters check them and replace them if needed. Smoke detectors save lives.

    Include a smoke detectors clause in your contract, stating that tenants are responsible to maintain them with fresh batteries every six months.

- **Fixtures: Lighting and Other.** Add a clause stating that tenants are responsible for the care of lighting fixtures. After a few years of renting, you don't want to enter a newly vacant rental house to find light bulbs not working or fixtures that stopped working and they never reported it to you. Renters sometimes expect landlords to replace burned out light bulbs or batteries in smoke detectors (see smoke detectors) and if you stipulate in your contract that tenants are responsible for this you have avoided a dispute.

- **Rental Insurance.** Require tenants purchase renters insurance. It's a big deal. If tenants have a fire your insurance company service providers cannot even touch your renters' possessions – unless they carry renters insurance. Consider requiring tenants to carry rental insurance, if legal in your area.

    A possible source of renters insurance information would be your insurance company. Perhaps your insurance agent would be interested or willing to talk to your current tenants. Renters insurance is very economical.

Side Story

Tracy and Albert, who are well into their forties and definitely know how to maintain a home, rented a duplex from Mike/Elaine for nearly two years. A few months before their last lease was up, Tracy called and asked Mike to replace a light bulb in an overhead light. Mike explained that renters must replace their own light bulbs.

Months later when Tracy and Albert had moved out, Mike found the light bulb was never replaced and several smoke detectors were squeaking away because batteries had not been replaced.

Sadly, Tracy and Albert had left their family with less light – but also in danger because functioning smoke detectors could no longer work.

- **Any Breach of Contract.** Make it clear: Any breach of contract will be grounds for eviction, no matter how minor one breach or another may appear.

- **Binding Effect.** End your contract with the following: The covenants and conditions herein contained shall apply to and bind the heirs, legal representatives, and assigns of the parties hereto, and all covenants are to be construed as conditions of this lease.

Initial Walk-Through

Never ever give your new tenant keys to your rental property until they have completed an initial walk through of the property with you. You need your new tenant to see that the refrigerator, stove, sink, kitchen cupboards, and bathrooms are in working order and not damaged.

Clean Initial Walk-Through

We have started to include a cleanliness inspection, as a separate form at the same time as the initial walk-through.

Renters seem to notice everything about a rental unit when they move in, which is great. A separate walk-through form, addressing the cleanliness of mirrors, kitchen cabinets, appliances, and much more can really help renters evaluate what they are seeing.

Renters have rights

Tenants are renting a house from you, and it will be their home. You, as their landlord, must respect that.

Landlords have rights

Okay, you as landlord own the house itself and everything within it – closets to cupboards, furnace to floorings and it is your right to believe it will be returned to you in about the same condition.

Yes, there is a term called "normal wear and tear" which means your flooring will be walked upon and your appliances will be used. But you have the right to have your property not purposely damaged.

As property manager you also have the right to inspect the premises, but you must give your renters notice. If you believe it to be an emergency you can enter the rental home – but you must have a legitimate reason: like another renter has complained about water running into their home from this home or a neighbor has heard screaming from within the home. By the way, never hesitate to call the police. Don't endanger yourself by entering what you consider to be a risky or dangerous situation.

Back to your rights; you have them but don't abuse them.

Good tenants

Good tenants need to be appreciated by their landlords; but not too much or they may become another type of tenant.

Bad tenants

Hopefully your bad tenants are on a periodic tenancy, with a contract that runs month to month.

Hold off on offering a tenant you're not sure about a longer term lease. They may request it, but hold off on signing a longer lease. Sure, a longer term lease means they are obligated to rent your house for a longer period of time but you will have a more difficult time removing them from the premises if you start to have difficulty.

Simply deliver to your bad tenant an "end-of-lease notice" which notifies them when the lease is now ending. You must provide your bad tenant with this notice at least one month before you want them to vacate.

Don't point fingers at them or scold them. Simply let them know you no longer want to be their landlord. Just remember, give them at least a month probably more. Check with your state, you don't want to end up in court with a renter who refuses to leave, and you didn't give them enough notice. You can avoid this by giving them at least the legal length notice. We like to give bad tenants an even longer notice, six weeks if possible.

But be prepared, if your tenant was bad before they're now going to become worse. You can avoid more bad behavior on their part by showing you will not be intimidated and do not let them convince you to extend their stay another month. By extending their stay you are essentially voiding your "end-of lease notice."

Other tenants

Do you suspect other people or unauthorized pets—not on the lease—are residing with your tenant?

If so, you must take immediate action.

First, ask your tenant.

It may be their aunt and uncle who have just moved into the area from across the country.

Some landlords we know of require their tenants to fill out a form when they have family visiting. The form states who they are and confirms how long they will be residing at their rental property.

We think family and friends should be able to visit without getting approval from a landlord. But that's just our opinion. Guests should stay no longer than the length of a traditional vacation.

Change the lease

If you have a month-to-month or period lease that both tenant and landlord have signed, you cannot change the lease without giving notice. The length of notice may vary by state but it will usually be over a month before a new lease can replace an older lease.

Neither landlord nor tenant can just decide to change the lease. Proper notice must be given.

Possible reasons to change a lease are: adjustment in rent, removing or adding a tenant, changing a term of the lease like amount withheld for utilities.

Do you have a tenant, but no lease? If you choose, you can rent your unit without a lease. We're not sure why anyone would want to do this, but it's legal. In some states, a non-lease rental agreement falls under a periodic or month-to-month lease.

Even if nothing is written on paper a rental agreement exists. Change this, get a lease.

Change the tenants

We don't allow tenants to sublet the unit they rent from us, to anyone else.

First the new tenants would not have passed your application process, therefore you know nothing about them.

If friends or acquaintances of your current tenants want to rent from you, have them go through your application process.

Remember the application fee we suggest should require tenants to submit a fairly small amount for a credit check and the rest comes back to them in the form of reduced rent.

Don't let any adult move into your rental unit without successfully completing your application process and signing a new lease.

Change your rental property

Let's say you decide to sell your rental property. Either you want to buy a bigger property, smaller unit, or get out of the business entirely. As landlord and property owner you can do this by simply selling your rental property.

Out of courtesy, if you have good renters you may want to offer them the property first.

But basically you have the right to sell the property anytime you want.

What you cannot do is break the lease between you and your tenants. Legally binding, a new property owner is bound by the same lease you have with a current tenant.

If it's simply a month to month lease you only have to give the same notice as you would for a change in lease. If it's a definite length, longer term lease then the property's new owner will have to respect the lease length.

An option would be for the new owner/landlord to offer a buyout to your current renter.

With a buyout, an agreed upon amount of money is offered to the current tenant. Renter would have to agree to leave, and be required to vacate the premises no later than an agreed upon date.

Update your rental property

Because your rental property is also your investment consider updating the unit. Painting walls should usually only be done between renters, when the unit is unoccupied. But you could update the landscaping, repair or replace old or chipped sidewalks, upgrade services, or replace siding.

Tenants appreciate landlords who take care of their rental property.

Between tenants you need to do some form of "rehabbing" where you patch holes in the wall and return your rental property to a habitable state. This would not be considered remodeling.

Remodeling would be updating the home's style using paint, new fixtures, and updated appliances. Perhaps even rooms could be laid out differently for a more modern feel. Remodeling would be totally deductible for you, even though they increase the value of your property.

Do remember, you could consider passing on at least part of these expenses to your new tenants. New tenants, viewing a newly updated home would likely not have a problem paying more rent for a home of quality.

Do not expect tenants to reside in a property that is going through a remodeling project which causes your renters distraction, annoyance, or interruption. The best time for a major remodeling would be between tenants.

Side Story

Mike/Elaine discovered, via tenant complaints, that the rental home's well water quality had diminished. After research they found a water system that would take care of the problem. But the system cost thousands of dollars and would require additional upkeep.

Rather than lose good tenants, Mike/Elaine purchased the system and took on the additional upkeep. Next time the tenant lease was up for renewal Mike/Elaine had to remind the good tenants why their monthly rent had to be increased slightly.

It's smarter to update for current good renters that you'd like to keep, than lose them and start again.

Landlords at rental property

Do not step onto your rental property unless you have a professional purpose for being there. Tenants have paid you money to temporarily call your investment property their home. Respect that.

But if you suspect there is illegal activity occurring on the premises you have both the legal right and perhaps even obligation, to check out the activities on your rental property.

Be prepared, you may have to legally defend your actions in a court of law, so make sure your reasons are legitimate.

Tenants at landlord's other property

Landlords have a right to their privacy. Some landlords do not want their tenants to know where they live. That's a personal choice.

Landlords do have another property. The property is called home. We feel it's not the worst thing in the world for your tenants to know where you live. What you want to avoid is renters thinking it's okay to drop by and see you whenever they like. If you find a tenant showing up in your driveway, or your yard, be friendly but keep it professional. Ask them what's going on, showing concern in your voice.

If they're good tenants they will realize they've crossed a boundary and excuse themselves soon. If they linger and don't get the idea, it is not beyond your options to tactfully state you have to leave soon implying they will want to leave too. If they continue to hang around, find an excuse to leave. You could say you've got to go shopping and then do it. Just be courteous...

Landlord Line

Say *"It was nice seeing you, I'll come over tomorrow afternoon at 5:00 and fix your leaky faucet. We're leaving to run some errands now, bye!"* Briefly visit with tenants who drop by your home unannounced but make sure they know you have other plans. Then go do those other plans or just take a short drive.

Side Story

Before Mike/Elaine stopped accepting rent payments at their home—the first evening of the month would find them with up to three different renters delivering their rent payments up until midnight!

Tenant Tip

Consider a post office box or another alternative mailing address where the tenants can not deliver their rent payments directly to you, their landlord. Not only encouraging them to submit their monthly rent on time, you will not have to deal with last-minute or late-night rent payment deliveries.

Part 2 : DURING renters

Have you covered all these topics? If not, review this list until you are comfortable with your decisions. Are you ready for tenants?

- ❏ New renters
- ❏ Friendly not friends
- ❏ Application process
- ❏ Application Form
- ❏ Credit Check
- ❏ Reference Check
- ❏ Put it in writing
- ❏ Periodic tenancy/ Month-to-month
- ❏ Definite-Term tenancy
- ❏ Lease
- ❏ Take the Time
- ❏ Initial Walk-Through
- ❏ Clean Initial Walk-Through
- ❏ Renters have rights
- ❏ Landlords have rights
- ❏ Good tenants
- ❏ Bad tenants
- ❏ Other tenants
- ❏ Change the lease
- ❏ Change the tenants
- ❏ Change your rental property
- ❏ Update your rental property
- ❏ Landlords at rental property
- ❏ Tenants at landlord's other property

DURING
renters

DURING renters

DURING
renters

DURING renters

DURING
renters

DURING
renters

Part 3
AFTER renters

Unexpected End of Lease

Tenants vacating before the end of a lease can be extremely rare; if you have chosen carefully it may never happen. Yet, landlords should be prepared for anything, when it comes to renters. Though uncommon, we've had leases unexpectedly end from silly to serious reasons.

Two weeks after new tenants moved into one of our duplex units, the renters in the adjoining unit called us to say that the new tenants were moving out and, in their words, "They had a big fight last night." The police had been called, but no one had called us.

We drove to the duplex and found out the rest of the story. One tenant had filed police charges the night before - as a result of the "big fight" and the other tenant was removing their possessions. Did the two-week-long tenants think about calling the landlord? No, they had not even considered it.

Tenants could leave—without your knowledge—in the middle of the night, or middle of a Sunday afternoon, as these two did to us.

Relationships change, situations occur, tempers can flare, and it can all occur in your investment property.

Side Story

Mike/Elaine have learned that being a landlord can be a tough job. Sometimes you are faced with difficult situations, especially when a lease ends unexpectedly.

To keep your sanity, remind yourself that being a landlord is just a job title. Sometimes you can help others, sometimes not.

But sometimes tenants are not in control of their choices: they are victims of violence. As a landlord you may be faced with legal issues and difficult situations.

Landlord Line

Remember, you are simply the landlord. Most business ventures have some level of risk and investment property is no different. Criminals-to-be may become your tenants with situations as diverse as government fraud, harboring fugitives, or murderers to be. We've had all. Your number one priority is the safety and well being of your tenants and to choose wisely so they don't become a danger in the neighborhood. But sometimes they have put themselves at risk and you simply need to deal with the aftermath.

A new tenant had signed a lease with us. A week before move-in date the tenant was murdered by another person who was also on the same lease. Their new lease, with us, had been signed. Neither had a previous criminal background.

No one contacted us until we called the [dead] tenant's cell phone for more information regarding their chosen move-in date.

We were very saddened by the death.

Legally, you need to check with your state regarding regulations when the death of a tenant is involved. Even though the tenant had not moved in, a lease had been signed and a deposit submitted.

In our state, if a tenant dies, the estate owes the next two months of rent. After the two months, the lease is nullified because the tenant is deceased.

As landlords we could have requested more money, but we did not. Check with your state regarding unexpected tenant departures, including deaths. You also need to realize that if a crime has taken place on your property, whether or not it results in a loss of income for you—your rental unit is now a crime scene.

If this occurs, check with your insurance company to see if you can possibly receive financial compensation for your loss in rental income. Insurance plans can include loss-of-rent benefits only when the premises involve a "loss of use."

If a crime has occurred within your rental property and the police require you to leave the unit vacant, your insurance company will likely not compensate you. However if the crime involves an "insurable act" which could cover blood stains or damage requiring repair, then you may receive insurance benefits because of "loss of use." Basically if you need to clean or repair the unit before it is rentable, you may receive insurance benefits for loss of rent.

If a tenant does voluntarily choose to break your lease and depart unexpectedly you can sue them for loss of rental payments they may owe you—until the end of your current lease.

If you had a month-to-month lease, you may only expect compensation for one full month after the current month. Even though they did not give you an end-of-lease notice the fact that they are gone pretty much tells you they don't want to be your tenant any more. Correct?

If you had a definite-term lease, you can expect full compensation for all unpaid rents. You may consider suing in small claims court or you may consider a collections agency.

We used to sue in small claims court and even though we won every judgement we have not recovered anything. Right, we said nothing.

Currently we turn all our tenants who have left owing us money over to a collections agency. The agency tells us that if we have a signed contract then we have the right to turn the money owing tenant over to a collections agency.

Check your state's regulations. Collection agency results may vary but the next time your money owing tenant applies to rent another home, buy a car, or even purchase a home—the collection will appear on their credit check. The local-level collection agency we use has

Side Story

Mike/Elaine had signed a lease with tenants who moved in but left the next day. They had excuses, but nothing legal. With over six months remaining on the lease Mike/Elaine had legal rights only until the unit was re-rented. You are legally obligated to try and find a new tenant, but your former tenant must compensate you for lost rental income.

Tenant Tip

It's not a good feeling to turn a former tenant who owes you money over to a collections agency. But consider that the tenant made a choice to leave owing you money.

told us individuals owing past landlords monies have paid what they owe up to seven years later. The past tenants decided to become homeowners and they had to resolve their debt.

Perhaps you too will eventually be paid by your gone—but not forgotten—tenant, and so will we!

Reason to end a Lease

You may end a lease by not renewing a current lease, or terminating an existing contract. As a landlord, you can end a lease for any number of legal reasons, as long as discrimination is not involved.

You cannot end a lease for any of the following reasons regarding the tenant or any legal tenant on your lease:

- Race
- Color
- Religion
- Sex
- Handicap
- Familiar Status
- National Origin

You may end a lease because you need to raise the rent and the tenant has already told you they cannot pay more rent, the tenant has breached one clause or more in your contract, or any other reason as long as you are not discriminating against the current tenant.

Unless we have a verbal communication problem with tenant, we like to discuss our end of lease decision with the tenant on the phone or in person. If you have had a courteous relationship with the tenant consider ending the tenancy on the same terms.

If your lease is month-to-month the length of time—before moveout date—may vary. We have found a month and one day written notice is acceptable. Check with your state as your state guidelines may vary. If you have no written lease with your tenant you may find the month-to-month rental guidelines may apply: legally you should not just walk up to your tenant and verbally tell them to leave.

A month-to-month lease means that neither landlord nor tenant have a legal obligation to continue your residential lease. Remember that if it is not working out you can end the lease.

Keep it a business relationship, not personal.

Landlord Line

Start with a month-to-month lease. State you have found it gives both the tenant and landlord a chance to know each other without a long-term commitment. The tenant has an opportunity to check out the home and the area by residing at the premises for a few months. If we find our landlord/tenant relationship is good we will usually offer a definite-term lease.

Sometimes the tenant asks for a definite-term lease, other times the tenant is not interested. Simply state, "Let's get to know each other first."

With a definite-term lease make sure your lease is specific on contract end date. If your tenant wants to continue to lease with you, offer a new contract at least one month and one day before the current lease ends. We like to have a new contract signed six weeks or more before current lease ends. It helps to avoid any problems or concerns at the last minute.

If a definite-term lease is going to expire with the landlord and/or tenant choosing not to create a new lease we suggest sending an end of notice document at least a month and one day before the definite lease is set to end.

Even though landlord and tenant may have a verbal agreement, putting it in writing is a good legal way to avoid unexpected problems. Consider that a tenant may find their life situation has changed and they simply want to stay. You may have to evict them. We'll cover evictions later, they are never fun, even if you win.

Side Story

Mike/Elaine had signed a month-to-month lease with Rory. A single mother with children in their mid-teens to early twenties, Rory's credit check was adequate. As the only adult tenant residing full time at the duplex unit, Rory was the only responsible party. Mike/Elaine wanted a longer term commitment from Rory and repeatedly asked her to sign a definite term lease.

Mike/Elaine's goals included asking Rory's adult children to sign a lease, but the subject was not broached because Rory refused to sign a new lease. It had also become apparent that Rory no longer lived full time within the unit and our other tenants were complaining of loud parties from Rory's children and their guests.

With no other choice, Mike/Elaine gave Rory an end-of-lease notice. When offered a long-term lease Rory still refused. Rory said "I don't want the commitment." But we did. So long Rory.

End-of-Lease Notice

To end a lease, either the landlord or tenant needs to deliver a written/printed notice to the other party.

Regulations vary state to state, but we have found that even though landlords have a signed lease with a tenant, it's best to deliver a letter stating you are ending a lease between you and your tenant. If multiple tenants are on your lease, you need to deliver a notice to each tenant.

Your notice should include the moveout date (last day of tenancy) and offer a final walk-through schedule. You may consider having the soon-to-be-gone tenant sign the end of lease notice, showing that they have received and acknowledged delivery of the letter. If your tenant is not happy about being asked to leave, they may not like being required to sign the letter. You may prefer to send the notice by registered U.S.P.S. (United States Postal Service) delivery or simply hand-deliver it yourself.

Keep the letter simple, but if the tenant has verbally told you that they must leave, because of a job loss or other circumstances you may want to include text that shows the tenant has chosen to end the lease. If you have had a good relationship between landlord and tenant, try to end on nice terms.

Lease End

You need to end a rental lease in a professional manner. If you have had a periodic tenancy which is a month-to-month lease, contract period end may occur within a short period of months or after many years.

Though we don't offer a clause covering renters who wish to break their lease for a move to another part of the country or to purchase a home, you may consider the option of offering renters a buyout. A buyout requires a tenant to submit a fee and they can break their lease before its natural end.

A buyout is not a breach of lease but a legal early ending of a lease. A common buyout amount is two months rent; it is never cheap for the tenant.

However you end the lease, make sure you act appropriately.

Renters have certain expectations like receiving their security/damage deposit back - with interest if required by your state statutes and if they've been good renters they hope you'll give them a good reference if they should apply for another rental home.

Landlord expectations are to have their rental unit returned to them in a reasonable manner. Normal wear and tear should be allowed, but that is sometimes a tough compromise between former tenant and former landlord.

Eviction

Eviction is a dirty word, for everyone.

Eviction can occur because a renter refuses to pay the agreed upon monthly rent or has breached your lease in some manner.

Legally, you cannot evict anyone. You cannot push them out of your rental property. What you can do, is file a request for an eviction or an "eviction action."

You must schedule a court hearing and request that a preceding judge determine that an eviction can occur. Then a police officer, or independent contractor you have hired, needs to serve the eviction.

Sometimes, we have found the most practical option is to try to work out your differences with your current tenant. If they agree to leave, you may have saved yourself money.

Unfortunately some tenants may agree to leave, just so you'll go away!

They plan to vacate when they are good and ready. At least try to negotiate if a peaceful resolution can occur. If your renter has shared with you that they have financial difficulties

Side Story

Mike/Elaine's only failed eviction was against their last Section 8 tenant. The seated judge did not even give Mike/Elaine a valid reason for the Section 8 renter to stay. As a Section 8 tenant when Mike/Elaine presented their evidence to Section 8 administration they dropped the tenant from their program.

Then Mike/Elaine had to start the eviction process again! Thankfully the tenant left before Mike/Elaine had to file an Eviction Action.

you can choose to allow a tenant to stay rather than evict them. The goal would be to work out a compromise. We have tried this with various renters but with absolutely no success.

Eventually we've had to evict. You could evaluate if the tenant situation will improve.

One time we tried mediation, because it was available and the bad tenants seemed to want to continue their rental agreement with us.

The bad renters found mediation to be another environment where they could blame everyone else for their problems. The plus side of mediation was that the bad renters voluntarily left. At mediation they signed a legal document agreeing to leave. They left mediation angry, but they were gone without an eviction.

If you must though, file an eviction action.

We give renters a three-day notice to resolve the unpaid rent, breach of lease, or whatever caused the eviction to be necessary.

Legally you may have to wait a longer time to evict someone, so make sure to check with your state statutes.

We like the three-day notice. It's enough time for renters to reconsider the route they are choosing to take and it may save you the eviction action.

Unlawful Detainer

Unlawful detainer, commonly referred to as a UD, is a legal term that means someone is accused of holding someone else's property without legally having possession of it.

Basically this is what happens when a legal court system has determined that a former tenant of yours is retaining possession of your rental property without authorization.

Never ever determine this on your own.

You must accuse the former renter within a court system and have a summons delivered to the renter. You will be required to show justification for the accusation of unlawful detainer.

If the person or persons occupying your rental property without your authorization have not paid rent or have breached your contract, and have been lawfully evicted in a court of law, then you can have an UD (Unlawful Detainer) served.

Depending on how your state statutes state the procedure, a sheriff may first post an unlawful detainer notice. Then, after a period of time determined by your state law, the sheriff may enter the premises and forcibly remove your unauthorized rental property occupant.

On top of that, the sheriff may also remove all their possessions and store them. The owner of the possessions may have to pay for the cost of removal of the property and storage fees if they want their possessions back.

State statutes are subject to change. Make sure to check your state legal procedures before you start any actions against a renter.

Hopefully you never have to file an unlawful detainer, but eventually you may find it unavoidable.

Court

You or your former renter may decide to sue each other. A common term for the type of court you will be summoned to is a conciliation court.

If your former tenant sues you they could be demanding all or part of their security deposit back, possessions they claim they left in the premises, or many more charges than we can even imagine.

Be prepared to support your actions within our legal system.

Your state may have a requirement regarding how long you have to return security/damage deposit or other deposits to your former tenants. Legal fines may be incurred if you do not correspond with your former tenants

and return any monies due in an appropriate length of time. These fines can be double the original amount or more. It's your investment, do not treat it lightly or you will find yourself losing what you planned to be a gain.

Good tenants leave

Renters who have been good tenants can be like good friends; you're sad when they move away. But you go on living.

Do consider if you like the tenant, and the feeling is mutual, you could begin a friendship with your former good tenant.

Wait until the tenant has become a former tenant and then send a note or email. Simply mention that you would like to continue the relationship.

Leave it up to the former tenant.

Bad tenants leave

Renters who have been bad can leave just that in your mouth - a bad taste.

Don't renew a lease with a renter with whom you have had problems. Don't be intimidated. It is your rental property and if someone is not paying their rent, taking care of your rental unit, or shows you they don't respect or want to follow your regulations, then you need to sever your relationship with them as soon as you legally can.

Bad tenants—left to their ways—will only get worse. Trust us, we've seen it happen.

Other tenants leave

Like we've mentioned elsewhere in *First-Time Landlord*, do not accept tenants who are not on your lease. Require them to leave.

You do not have to speak to the additional tenants who are not on your lease. Your problem isn't with them, it's with your tenant who is allowing them to reside illegally in your investment property. Never forget that.

Consider it dangerous to confront someone you do not know in an assertive manner. Because you do not know this person, or persons, there is no knowing how they will react.

Discuss your concerns about the illegal tenants, with the renters with whom you have a lease. If you don't have personal contact with your renters, notify them with a breach of lease notice.

Require them to have the other tenants leave, or warn your renter that you will be required to file for an eviction action.

Remember you must have proof of the other unauthorized tenants. This could be photographs, if acceptable in court, or other renters who have witnessed the other unauthorized tenants on the premises at times of the day/evening that would show they live at the property.

It is illegal for you to open your tenant's mailbox and check for mail addresses to find unauthorized tenants who are using your rental address as their own.

You could talk with your other tenants or neighbors—another time when it comes in handy to be on friendly terms with your rental property neighbors. Perhaps they would be willing to help you remove unauthorized tenants. It is their neighborhood, if you show that you care they will likely care about you.

Your local police department may not be able to help you, but Mike recommends becoming known at the police precinct that serves your rental property.

If the police know you care—guess what—they will probably care too!

No forwarding address

Remind tenants—whenever possible—that you must know their forwarding address to receive their security/damage deposit, plus interest.

Tenants should leave you a forwarding address. We require tenants to print their forwarding address—where they next plan to live or are already living—on the back of our Final Walk-Through.

Because it is on the same form as their final walk-through it may serve as legal evidence if you should go to court or collections.

If tenants have not left you a forwarding address you can address mail to their last known place of residency: your rental unit. Unless they are avoiding having their mail forwarded, the mail you have addressed to them should be forwarded to them at their next residency.

Final Walk-Through

When you deliver your end-of-lease notice, alert your soon-to-be former tenant that they are required to schedule a final walk-through with you. You have been holding their security/damage deposit—plus pet deposit if a pet was part of their lease—and they should be eager to get their deposit returned to them.

A final walk-through must occur when the tenant still has occupancy, during the rental time period. Always encourage renters to do the final walk-through while they still are in the property, so that they have time to correct any issues that concern you.

Remember, your last inspection of the rental home should be completed with the participation of your soon-to-be former renter.

If your former tenant does not appear for the scheduled final walk-through or does not stay, complete the final walk-through as if they were present.

Tenant Tip

In the last month of rental, deliver to the tenant a reminder that they need to complete a final walk-through with you.

Perhaps you'd prefer to set a time when you'll be at the property or require them to schedule an appointment with you. Final walk-throughs must be done, or the tenant may claim they left the unit in great shape.

Your final walk-through form is a legal document and you may need to use it as evidence in a court case or to a collections agency.

The only way they can get their security/damage deposit back is to return your rental unit to you, in a manner you find acceptable.

Some landlords don't care if the walls are clean or dirty. They simply plan to repaint between renters and don't care what condition the walls are in when the former renters leave.

But there's a catch here. If you keep repainting dirty walls the paint will eventually chip and peel off. Then the walls must be scraped, primed, and repainted.

You may want to discuss this with tenants, but be prepared that tenants may not recognize this as a problem. We have seen tenants leave their former home with beverage splashes on the walls and woodwork, with no sign of anyone even trying to wipe off the spills.

Seeing how some tenants left dirt and filth behind, we sometimes go in the following direction.

Point out to departing tenants all areas you will need to repair or replace because of their negligence. Except for your time (as property manger) all these expenses should be deductible from their security/damage deposit.

Final Clean Walk-Through

Tenants don't seem to notice the cleanliness conditions when they leave a rental unit, but they sure do when they move into a rental unit.

It's to your advantage to require tenants to leave a rental unit as clean

Side Story

Cindy seemed agreeable, as new renters usually do. During the Initial Walk-Through Cindy asked Mike if she could complete the walk-through later - and Mike agreed. Cindy never returned the completed Initial Walk-Through form. A year later Mike/Elaine had not asked Cindy to renew their contract and their Final Walk-Through needed to be completed. Cindy, in writing, asked Mike/Elaine for a copy of the Initial Walk-Through. That's when Mike realized he had never received it back from Cindy. Gladly the lack of a completed Initial Walk-Through did not become an issue, but neither Mike nor Elaine will ever leave a walk-through - again - without the form completed!

Side Story

Cindy and Elaine were walking through Cindy's former rental unit on the last evening of their rental contract. Elaine opened the stove and looked inside. It was covered with burnt food particles and a dirty film. Elaine looked at Cindy and asked if she considered the oven clean. Cindy calmly replied "It is as clean as I could get it without buying oven cleaner." Elaine responded "Right." Elaine offered Cindy the opportunity to clean it, but Cindy refused as she wanted to leave.

as they found it. A number of landlord guides simply require tenants to vacate the premises and clean the floors with a broom.

For landlords who complete their own property maintenance, or cannot afford an expensive cleaning crew to prepare a rental unit between renters, a clean walk-through has enormous benefit.

Reference Calls

During tenants' last few weeks in your rental home they may be searching for a new home. You may receive calls from potential landlords.

Answer questions, but keep your comments very brief. Privacy laws are involved so do not volunteer information. Keep your private feelings just that – to yourself. If you choose, refuse to answer. We don't know why you would refuse to answer, but maybe you only have bad things to say about this renter. Of course the landlord calling will wonder why you're not willing to give your comments, they can probably guess why you won't comment.

Potential landlords can ask the following:

- Do they pay their rent on time?
- Would you rent to them again?

Let's say your answers are:

- Yes.
- Yes.

Your conversation should be short and your current tenant will likely soon become their tenant. Remember you want good renters, so try to be as honest as possible.

Let's say your answers are:

- Yes.
- No.

You are stating, yes they pay their rent on time and no you would not rent to them again. Be careful what you say next, you can be sued for slander if you claim untruths about your renter. Sometimes, if it was nothing specific, we say it just wasn't a good fit. Let the inquiring landlord make their own decision about what you mean. Former tenants may or may not choose to use you as a reference, but a history check will show you as their landlord. You may receive a phone call if your tenant has filled out a new application. Legally, you can and should say very little.

In review:
You will be asked: if your renter paid on time and if you would rent to them again. Answer those questions, as briefly as possible. You should never volunteer information about a current or former tenant as they have a legal right to their privacy.

Questions you cannot answer, if you are asked include:

- Was your former renter friendly?
- Too many parties?
- Too many loud parties?
- Do you consider them to lead a moral life?

If you are asked any personal questions, don't answer. Renters have a right to their privacy.

We are not offering you legal advice, for more information seek legal council. But remember people have been sued for stating falsehoods or sharing private information.

Follow-Up Letter

We recommend a follow-up letter to your former tenants, as soon as possible after their move-out date. A follow-up letter can cover multiple issues: return of deposits and unresolved expenses regarding the rental time period. Let's cover security/damage deposits first.

Our state requires you contact your former tenant—in writing/print—no more than 21 days after they have vacated your rental property. The purpose of the letter is to inform your former tenant regarding the return of their security/damage deposit.

Tenants should have submitted a security/damage deposit before or upon the date they took possession of your rental property. If for some reason, they did not submit a deposit, you need to check with legal counsel regarding any necessary follow-up contact you may need with your former tenant.

You are legally required to return your former tenants security/damage deposit minus any legible legal sums they owe to you—and you must do so within a timely fashion.

Side Story

Mike/Elaine received a phone message asking for a reference regarding a former renter, Jack. Elaine returned the call and was surprised that Jack had used them as a reference. A few years had passed since Jack had been a tenant of Mike/Elaine's and he had not been a great one. The potential landlord/property manager explained that Jack had not given out Mike/Elaine as part of his address history, but they had completed more intensive research. Back to the two simple questions: had Jack paid the rent on time and would we rent to him again. Two simple negative responses from Elaine and another landlord was going to pass on Jack. Tell the truth and don't explain more than is needed.

If your former tenants owe you more than the amount they originally deposited with you, consider suing them in conciliation court. If you owe tenants any deposit amount and do no return their funds in a timely manner, they may sue you in conciliation court.

We'll discuss security/damage deposits and incurred interest next, but first we'd like to explain why we do not return security/damage deposits immediately.

We use the follow-up letter to remind tenants we will not be automatically returning their security/damage deposit and interest because our contracts require our tenants to be responsible for their own utilities [authors note: refer to utilities incentive.] Departing tenants are not likely to voluntarily submit any additional sums to you, so make sure they do not owe you any additional amounts before returning their remaining deposits.

Whether or not you need to retain the departing tenants' deposits you must contact them. You have to legally let them know when, or if, you are returning any portion of their security/damage deposit. You also need to support why you are retaining any funds.

Return of Security/Damage Deposit

First you must total all the deposit-type sums your former tenant submitted to you. If you required separate deposits for residence, another for garage, another for storage unit, and/or another for pet damage deposit you should add them together.

If you can document the dates you received these amounts, that would be helpful. We document all deposits as part of our lease.

Let's use an example: your departing tenant submitted $1,000.00.

Return of Security/Damage Deposit Interest

It's simple.

Legally, you may need to pay interest to departing tenants, based upon the total sum of the security/damage deposits they submitted to you.

The amount of interest you calculate, if any, will be stipulated by your state laws. Usually we have found it to be a flat rate, like 3%, 2%, or 1%. Check statutes on a regular basis, as state regulations can and do change.

We calculate the interest first, before we move on to any possible deductions. We find it to be most fair to tenants and shows a sign of good will on your part as their former landlord.

Using our previous example of $1,000.00 and an interest rate of 1% the total sum now due to your departing tenant would be $1,010.00. Initial deposit was $1,000.00 to which we added $10.00 incurred interest.

Deductible Expenses

After adding interest to departing tenants' security/damage deposit you should next consider any outstanding expenses. If monthly rent has included all utilities and departing tenant has left rental property in acceptable condition you should next write out a check to departing tenant.

In our continuing example, the check amount would be $1,010.00. Make sure to note on check face—and any accompanying letter—that check is reimbursement of entire security/damage deposit. Mail reimbursement check, and any letter, to address tenant gave you during their final walk-through.

Out-of-pocket expenses—not covered under normal wear and tear—may be costs you can deduct from departing tenants' security/damage deposit.

Following would be possible deductible expenses:

- unpaid utilities covering time period tenant had possession of unit including but not limited to gas, electric, water, sewer, city or other utilities,

- damage to rental unit not covered by normal wear and tear (make sure you document damage during final walk-through) including broken windows, built-in cabinets pulled from their locations, or fixtures,

- repair of any tenant unauthorized alterations to rental unit (make sure you document unauthorized alterations during final walk-through) which could include dismantle or install permanent fixtures,

alter woodwork or carpet, paper or paint walls, or any other area that will need to be restored to pre-tenant possession condition,

- replacement/repair of rental property unlawfully damaged or destroyed by tenant (make sure you document unauthorized alterations during final walk-through)

Remember tenant is responsible for all unauthorized damages (beyond normal wear and tear) which occur within or on premises of rental unit even if they themselves did not cause the damage. That means even if the tenant did not cause the damage they are responsible.

Let's take another look at our example. Departed tenants' security/damage deposit plus incurred interest of $1,010.00 remains but in final walk-through some damage is discovered:

	$1,010.00	Deposit plus interest
-	225.00	Stove damaged by tenant
	$785.00	

After replacing stove damaged by tenant (see Side Story) remainder of sum owed to tenant would be mailed to departed tenant at their new residence.

Before you consider new tenants

You always have choices but between tenants is an excellent time to consider your options. Perhaps your personal situation has changed: you've married or divorced, switched or lost a full-time job, or want to make changes to how you handle your investment properties.

A possible option would be to sell your investment property to one of your tenants either on a contract for deed or through a conventional bank loan or mortgage. Always consider any further legal issues.

But you need to keep in mind that your commitment to tenants is to provide a safe and secure home for the renters who have signed a contract with you.

Side Story

Elaine and Wendy were completing Wendy's final walk-through. Elaine noticed there was a problem with the oven door. Pulling it open and shut, the right side would not seal. After a discussion with Wendy it was clear that Wendy's teen-age son had stood on the oven door, while it was open. The stove would not longer seal and it had to be replaced.

Landlord Line

You are a landlord: you are responsible for the safety, security, and comfort level of your tenants while they are within the home they rent from you.

We had furnace trouble. We called in a local contractor who lied to us and told us our furnace was "bad" and we needed to replace it.

With tenants you need to keep your own personal finances in order so you are prepared to provide for your renters.

We sat in chilly weather for five days while considering our options. A trusted family member looked at our furnace and found it needed a 15-minute cleaning. It was not broken. Catch is, if it's your tenant you don't have five days to think about anything. You need to repair or replace anything vital to a home. Consider that tenant concerns need to be your priority.

As a landlord state to your tenants, "I'll fix or replace it immediately."

As landlord you are allowing someone to use your investment property on a temporary basis, for a sum of money.

Remember in Part 1: BEFORE Renters when we discussed stocks? Your investment is in "stock"—your rental property. Let your rental property earn profit for you. Just don't forget your tenant, the source of your earnings!

In Closing

If you choose to become a landlord we believe you may be making a sound investment and offering a vital service to your community.

Consider your personality, situation, and finances. Would you make a good first-time landlord?

Good luck and feel free to contact us,
Mike and Elaine McManigle!
landlordbook@wencl-creative.com

Part 3 : AFTER renters

Have you covered all these topics? If not, review this list until you are comfortable with your decisions.

- ❏ Unexpected end of Lease
- ❏ Reason to end a Lease
- ❏ End of Lease Notice
- ❏ Lease End
- ❏ Eviction
- ❏ Unlawful Detainer
- ❏ Court
- ❏ Good tenants leave
- ❏ Bad tenants leave
- ❏ Other tenants leave
- ❏ No forwarding address
- ❏ Final Walk-Through
- ❏ Final Clean Walk-Through
- ❏ Reference Calls
- ❏ Follow-Up Letter
- ❏ Return of Security/Damage Deposit
- ❏ Return of Security/Damage Deposit Interest
- ❏ Deductible Expenses
- ❏ In Closing

AFTER
renters

AFTER
renters

AFTER
renters

AFTER
renters

AFTER
renters

AFTER
renters

First-Time Landlord: Index

Symbols
28 or 29 days 60
30 days 60
31 days 60

A
advantage 55, 91
advertise 26, 28, 34
after 9, 10, 16, 30, 33, 35, 47, 51
another form of insurance 37
apartment 20, 21, 22, 23
applicant 7, 28, 29, 31, 32, 46, 47, 48, 49, 50, 51, 52, 56, 58, 59
application 7, 26, 27, 29, 37, 46, 47, 49, 57, 72, 93
appointment 31, 32, 90
assistance 33, 48

B
backup plan 47
before 1, 9, 10, 12, 14, 16, 18, 19, 27, 34, 35, 46, 52, 53, 55, 56, 57, 58, 60, 61, 65, 67, 68, 69, 87
building 20, 21, 22, 23, 24, 29, 54

C
cardboard box 35
casual 32
cat 30
clean 1, 17, 24, 62
coin-operated 20, 24
color 28, 82
commitment 36, 48, 49, 50, 54, 55, 57, 58, 84, 94
components of an application form 48
computer 26
connection 25, 27, 34, 50
contract 2, 18, 33, 34, 35, 36, 53, 55, 56, 57, 58, 60, 63, 65, 66, 67, 81, 82, 83, 84, 87, 91, 93, 94
court 33, 37, 68, 71, 81, 85, 86, 87, 89, 90, 91
credit check 47, 49, 51, 52, 57, 58, 69, 81, 84
cringe 29

D
deadline 58
definite-term 54, 57, 72
deposit 30, 34, 35, 36, 58, 59, 80, 85, 87, 90, 91
disadvantage 18, 22, 24
disruptive 22, 24, 62
distance 15, 17, 18, 21
dog 29, 30, 59
drug use 11
duplex 17, 18, 49, 65, 79, 84
duplicate check 59, 60
during 45, 72, 90

E

Elaine 2, 3, 4, 7, 8, 9, 10, 11, 12, 17, 18, 22, 29, 30, 31, 32, 33, 34, 36, 37, 45, 46, 49, 53, 55, 58, 59, 62, 65, 79, 81, 84, 85, 91, 93, 94
eviction 37, 85, 86, 89
excuse 37, 49, 71

F

fair housing regulation 27
familiar Status 28, 82
fee 46, 51, 52, 57, 59, 60, 61, 69, 84
fight 79
final walk-through 90, 91, 95
first-time 2, 11, 27, 52, 88
flippant 32
four-plex 20
friend 48, 53, 55
friendly 8, 10, 45, 71, 89, 93
fun 31, 83
furnace 22, 66, 94

G

garden 22, 23

H

fandicap 28, 82

I

illegal 17, 22, 51, 63, 71, 89
important 22, 25, 32
income 2, 3, 11, 12, 20, 24, 28, 50, 52, 80, 81
information 11, 14, 16, 19, 25, 33, 48, 50, 51, 52, 58, 65
inspection 63, 90
insurance 2, 19, 26, 33, 36, 37, 38, 59, 65, 80, 81
internet access 26

L

landlord 2, 7, 9, 10, 11, 27, 30, 37, 38, 45, 52, 56, 71, 79, 80, 82, 83, 84, 85, 91, 92, 93, 94
landlord line 7, 30, 37, 56, 71, 80, 83, 94
last month's rent 35, 36, 37, 38, 58
late 59, 60, 61
laundry 20, 22, 23, 24
lease 7, 33, 34, 35, 36, 55, 79
legal 2, 3, 14, 19, 33, 36, 48, 49, 50, 51, 52, 54, 59, 62, 64, 65, 66, 68, 71, 80, 81, 82, 83, 85, 86, 87, 89, 90, 91, 93
list 6, 49
listen 29, 38, 46
loud parties 24, 84, 93

M

mailbox 89
Mike/Elaine 2, 7, 8, 9, 10, 11, 17, 18, 22, 29, 30, 32, 33, 34, 36, 37, 49, 53, 55, 59, 62, 65, 79, 81, 84, 85, 91, 93
military 30
money 2, 3, 5, 6, 11, 12, 14, 20, 22, 24, 34, 35, 37, 57, 58, 70, 71, 80, 81, 85, 94
month-to-month 35, 53, 54, 57, 59, 68, 69, 81, 82, 83, 84
multi-unit 20, 22

N
national origin 28, 82
neighbor 14, 17, 25, 67
new tenant 57, 66, 69, 80, 81, 83
nicer 29
no forwarding address 90, 95
not paid 87
no written contract 53

O
occupant 47, 87
one-bedroom 28
out-of-pocket expense 1
overpaid 34

P
paint 91
payment 15, 22, 27, 37, 51, 58, 59, 60, 61
periodic tenancy 33, 57, 84
pet 30, 90
pet damage deposit 30
petty 18
police 11, 18, 22, 25, 33, 67, 79, 81, 85, 89
potential renter 35, 36, 37
potential tenant 59
professional 8, 9, 14, 45, 50, 51, 52, 71, 84
property 1, 2, 3, 4, 5, 6, 7, 8, 9, 11, 12, 13, 14, 15, 16, 17, 18, 19, 20, 21, 22, 23, 24, 25, 26, 29, 31, 32, 33, 35, 36, 38, 46, 79, 80, 81, 86, 87, 88, 89, 90, 91, 93, 94
property maintenance 1, 2, 38, 91
property management 2, 57, 58
Property management 2, 38

Q
quit 24, 64

R
race 82
realtor 2, 25
reference calls 92, 95
religion 28, 82
renter 2, 7, 11, 14, 17, 18, 19, 20, 21, 22, 24, 25, 29, 30, 33, 35, 36, 37, 54, 85, 86, 87, 88, 89, 90, 92, 93
renters insurance 36, 37, 38, 65
repaint 91
reputation 24
research 14, 20, 26, 93
respect 6, 22, 25, 63, 66, 70, 88
responsible 5, 15, 16, 19, 20, 21, 22, 26, 33, 36, 48, 55, 56, 61, 65, 84
RHR Information Services 52
risky 12, 67

S

safe 4, 62
security/damage deposit 34, 35, 58, 59
sex 28, 82
shared 9, 17, 19, 23, 24, 35, 85, 87
side story 2, 3, 4, 7, 9, 11, 17, 18, 22, 24, 25, 29, 30, 32, 33, 36, 37, 45, 49, 53, 57, 58, 59, 62, 63, 65
signs 26, 64
single family 15, 38, 62
smoking 61
sound protection 22, 23
state statutes 86, 87
sublet 69

T

tax 3
tenant 47, 53, 54, 55, 56, 57, 58, 59, 61, 62, 63, 64, 66, 67, 68, 69, 70, 71, 79, 80, 81, 82, 83, 84, 85, 86, 87, 88, 89, 90, 92, 93, 94
tenant 1, 8, 10, 12, 14, 16, 28, 31, 34
tenant tip 1, 8, 10, 12, 14, 16, 28, 31, 34, 61, 81, 90
triplex 20

U

UD 58, 59, 86, 87
umbrella policy 26
unauthorized 87, 89
unexpected 79, 95
unexplained damage 2, 62
unit 1, 5, 7, 8, 10, 12, 13, 15, 16, 17, 18, 19, 20, 21, 22, 23, 24, 25, 28, 29, 30, 31, 32, 33, 34, 35, 38, 46, 47, 55, 57, 58, 61, 62, 66, 68, 69, 70, 79, 80, 81, 84, 85, 88, 89, 90, 91, 92
unlawful detainer 58, 86, 95
unpaid rent 86
untidy 23
utility 16, 17, 19, 21, 23, 34, 35
utility incentive 19, 34
utility use 23, 34

W

walk-through 66, 72, 91
warning 34, 53

Y

yard 15, 16, 17, 18, 21, 22, 45, 71
yard care 15, 16, 17, 22

Made in the USA
Lexington, KY
19 May 2014